BLUEPRINTS
Geography
Key Stage
Teacher's Resource
Book

Second Edition

Stephen Scoffham

Colin Bridge

Terry Jewson

Stanley Thornes (Publishers) Ltd

Do you receive **BLUEPRINTS NEWS?**

Blueprints is an expanding series of practical teacher's ideas books and photocopiable resources for use in primary schools. Books are available for separate infant and junior age ranges for every core and foundation subject, as well as for an ever widening range of other primary teaching needs. These include **Blueprints Primary English** books and **Blueprints Resource Banks**. **Blueprints** are carefully structured around the demands of National Curriculum in England and Wales, but are used successfully by schools and teachers in Scotland, Northern Ireland and elsewhere.

Blueprints provide:
- *Total curriculum coverage*
- *Hundreds of practical ideas*
- *Books specifically for the age range you teach*
- *Flexible resources for the whole school or for individual teachers*
- *Excellent photocopiable sheets – ideal for assessment and children's work profiles*
- *Supreme value.*

Books may be bought by credit card over the telephone and information obtained on **(01242) 577944**. Alternatively, photocopy and return this **FREEPOST** form to receive **Blueprints News**, our regular update on all new and existing titles. You may also like to add the name of a friend who would be interested in being on the mailing list.

Please add my name to the **BLUEPRINTS NEWS** mailing list.

Mr/Mrs/Miss/Ms _____

Home address _____

_____ Postcode _____

School address _____

_____ Postcode _____

Please also send **BLUEPRINTS NEWS** to:

Mr/Mrs/Miss/Ms _____

Address _____

_____ Postcode _____

To: Marketing Services Dept., Stanley Thornes Ltd, FREEPOST (GR 782), Cheltenham, GL50 1BR

First published in 1992 by:
Stanley Thornes (Publishers) Ltd
Ellenborough House
Wellington Street
CHELTENHAM GL50 1YD

Reprinted 1993 (twice), 1994

Second edition 1995

A catalogue record for this book is available from the British Library.

ISBN 0–7487–2210–6

Typeset by Tech Set Limited, Gateshead, Tyne & Wear
Printed in Great Britain at The Bath Press, Avon

CONTENTS

INTRODUCTION

What is *Blueprints Geography*?

Blueprints Geography Key Stage 1 has been devised to cover the requirements of the geography National Curriculum at Key Stage 1. It consists of this *Teacher's Resource Book*, which may be used independently, and an accompanying book of *Pupils' Copymasters*. It is intended for practising teachers, particularly non-specialists who may find themselves teaching geography for the first time or who are unsure how to approach the subject. Students and others who are involved with education will also find it invaluable.

The *Teacher's Resource Book* contains over 200 ideas and practical suggestions. These are developed and extended in the supporting book of *Pupils' Copymasters*. There is a strong emphasis on mapwork, fieldwork and practical enquiries. Special sections provide background information about two contrasting UK localities. Current teaching materials on distant places are also listed.

How is the *Teacher's Resource Book* organised?

The *Teacher's Resource Book* is divided into three main sections covering skills, places and themes. Each section begins with a general introduction and background notes. This then leads into a number of units based on the National Curriculum Orders. Additional sections at the front and back of the book deal with topic planning, progression and assessment.

What is the structure of each unit?

Each unit covers part of the Programme of Study and is presented in a similar way:

Tint panel – reproduces the requirements in the geography Orders.

Interpretation – gives a description of the activities the children might do.

Progression indicators – provide guidance on different levels of achievement and competence.

Introduction – sets out key geographical ideas within the unit.

Key vocabulary – ten to fifteen geographical terms which will support the children's learning.

Key questions – focus attention on enquiries and investigations.

Resources – songs, poems, stories and software which link to the unit.

Activities – up to a dozen activities for children to undertake involving fieldwork and research.

Copymasters – references to supporting copymasters in the Pupils' Copymaster book.

Blueprints links – links to other books in the Blueprints series.

How can I use Blueprints Geography?

Blueprints Geography is a flexible resource which can be consulted in a number of different ways:

1. You can work from the topic planners and web diagrams on pages vii-xviii. These have been selected to give full coverage of the geography programme of study and indicate opportunities for cross-curricular links.
2. You can identify areas of the Programme of Study which you wish to teach and turn directly to the appropriate unit.
3. You can select activities of your choice to support an individual teaching scheme. The topic planners and unit headings will help you to locate them easily.

How can I use the *Pupils' Copymasters*?

The *Pupils' Copymasters* book contains 118 copymaster sheets. Although you could complete the activities without using the copymasters, the copymasters will help you to develop the activities to their full potential. They also provide a structure for enquiries and fieldwork. This is something which is stressed in the National Curriculum Orders.

What records should I keep?

It is valuable to keep a record of the pupils' work so that you can monitor their progress. One way of doing this is to keep a folder for each child. The copymasters provide an ideal and easy way of building up a record of achievement.

How can I assess pupils' achievements in geography?

The level descriptions for use at the end of Key Stage 1 are reproduced at the back of this book. There are also portraits of what a typical child might be expected to achieve in each year group, and links to appropriate activities and copymasters. Non-specialists may find the progression indicators at the start of each unit in the main body of the book particularly helpful. These are a novel feature of the **Blueprints** series and show how children's learning can develop. You can use the indicators for differentiation, associate them with the topic planners for assessment and use them to help judge children's achievement at the end of the Key Stage.

Do I need any special resources?

You will need to build up a bank of resources in order to teach National Curriculum geography. Large scale Ordnance Survey maps of the local area are invaluable. Globes, atlases, photographs, fieldwork equipment and computer programs will also be required. There is a list of addresses of appropriate agencies and commercial suppliers on page 90. The resources required for each individual activity are also listed under the heading at the beginning of the activity.

COVERAGE OF THE CURRICULUM FOR SCOTLAND, WALES AND NORTHERN IRELAND

Blueprints: Geography Key Stage 1 covers most of the geography curriculum requirements in place for 5–7 year olds in Wales, Scotland and Northern Ireland. Most of the activities in the book are 'content-free' with regard to location and can easily be adapted to particular place studies and regional needs.

In the charts which follow we have set out the key curriculum content for the relevant stages for Northern Ireland and Scotland and you will find this cross-referenced to the activity numbers in the book. As the Welsh and English Orders are broadly similar, apart from the map which shows points of reference for Wales, Welsh teachers should find the structure of the book reasonably accessible. The copymasters which relate to particular activities will of course also be valuable.

LINKS TO THE SCOTTISH GUIDELINES 5–14 ▶

Environmental Studies
Social subjects: Understanding People and Place
Contexts and content for developing understanding
Stages P1 to P3

ASPECTS OF THE PHYSICAL AND BUILT ENVIRONMENT	ACTIVITIES
Different kinds of weather and simple weather recording	10, 201–211
Major physical and natural features in the locality	3–11, 96, 97

WAYS IN WHICH PLACES HAVE AFFECTED PEOPLE AND PEOPLE HAVE USED AND AFFECTED PLACES	ACTIVITIES
Our responses to weather variations, from day to day and season to season	212–218
The uses of buildings and land in the local area	13, 14, 19, 23, 183
Places used in the provision of services	92, 159–169
Some ways of maintaining a clean environment	137–146, 171, 175
Daily lives of children elsewhere compared with their own	102, 107, 110, 156, 218

LOCATIONS, LINKAGES AND NETWORKS	ACTIVITIES
Kinds of traffic in the area and the need for safety procedures	184–197
Boundaries and their importance for safety	28, 29
Things we use and eat which come from distant places	81, 104, 235

MAKING AND USING MAPS	ACTIVITIES
Developing the mental map of familiar places	24, 25, 55, 64, 90, 91
Making models of known places and story settings	57–60, 115, 149, 165
Using plans to find places	36, 45, 61, 62
Using the globe as a representation of the world	83, 113, 199

LINKS TO THE NORTHERN IRELAND CURRICULUM ▷

Key Stage 1

AT1 METHODS OF GEOGRAPHICAL ENQUIRY	ACTIVITIES
Environment	3–9, 24, 25
Simple relationships	26, 29, 32
Follow directions	38–43, 61, 62
Road safety	
Plan views	51–56, 149
Using keys	60
Different scales	63
Follow a route	42–47
Letter/number co-ordinates	82
Draw simple maps	57–60
Use compass points	48–50
Show relationships	96
Identify land and sea	82, 83

AT2 PHYSICAL ENVIRONMENTS	ACTIVITIES
Record the weather	201–211
Weather and living things	212–218
Different natural materials	225–239
Compare rocks	84
Action of wind and water	136
Soil composition	85, 86
Recognise habitats	142, 152
Identify landscape features	9

AT3 HUMAN ENVIRONMENTS	ACTIVITIES
Different jobs	170–183
Providing goods and services	159–167
Means of transport	184–200
Compare homes	150, 155, 156
Uses of buildings	19–21, 92
Size of settlements	80

AT4 PLACE AND SPACE	ACTIVITIES
Location on maps and globes	71
Boundaries	78, 79
Local features	84–97
Places in Northern Ireland	64
Places in British Isles	68, 69, 70
Frame of reference	63

AT5 ISSUES IN A CHANGING WORLD	ACTIVITIES
Issues which arise when individuals or groups have conflicting views on the use of resources	120, 125, 137, 138, 145, 146

PLANNING TOPICS

You can teach geography in a number of different ways. It can be delivered:

- as a subject in its own right;
- through topics which focus on geography but which also involve related elements from a limited number of other subjects;
- through 'broad topics' which integrate material in a structured way from a number of different subjects.

Most infant schools organise the curriculum through 'broad topics'. This means that geography is presented in a wide context.

The features which contribute to successful topic planning have been identified by OFSTED inspectors. These are:

1) A carefully structured planning system which helps to ensure continuity and progression
2) Co-operation between teachers so they share workload and expertise
3) Careful attention to national curriculum requirements
4) Topics which are focused either on a single subject or which emphasise particular subjects
5) Whole school agreement about the balance between subjects and topics
6) Plans which identify learning outcomes.

The programme of study for geography

Whatever approach you adopt, it is important to see that you obtain a broad and balanced coverage of the curriculum. The programme of study for geography is constructed around three different elements – skills, places and themes. Figure 1 summarises the require-

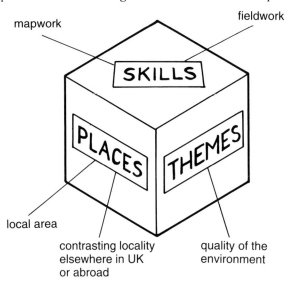

Figure 1 *The programme of study is constructed around skills, places and themes.*

ments at Key Stage 1. Any scheme of work will need to cover these different elements. It will also need to provide children with opportunities to ask geographical questions, collect evidence and draw conclusions from their findings.

Topic Planners 1–3

The planners in this section show how geography can be taught through focused topics. Each planner begins with a brief description of the topic and references to the Orders for geography and other related subjects. There is also a web diagram and a panel listing appropriate activities.

The planners begin with school locality and conclude with work on the environment. The topics have been presented in this order to match the increasing intellectual and emotional maturity of the children as they move through the year bands. (See Figure 2). However, you might decide to use the topics in a different order to match your school plan.

All three topics provide natural links with other subjects. Associations with art, music, science and history are highlighted in the planners. However, the opportunities for developing key skills in mathematics and English should not be overlooked. Geography is an

Reception	Year 1	Year 2
The local area	A contrasting locality	The environment

Figure 2 *The topics can be organised in a progressive way.*

ideal vehicle for illustrating ideas from the core curriculum. By making these connections it is possible to develop geographical studies alongside work on language and number, thereby reducing the pressure on the school timetable.

Topic planners 4—10

Schools that wish to integrate the curriculum through broad topics will find it useful to work from the planners in this section. The content has been selected to match the needs and understanding of pupils as they progress through the infant school. The focus is sufficiently general to permit connections between a large number of curriculum subjects. The planners give complete coverage of the geography and history curriculum and incorporate a considerable variety of scientific ideas. They also include references to art, music, design and technology, IT and PE. As the Orders for these subjects concentrate on skills and processes, your school will need to make decisions about the content which it considers to be most appropriate.

**Implementing national
curriculum geography**

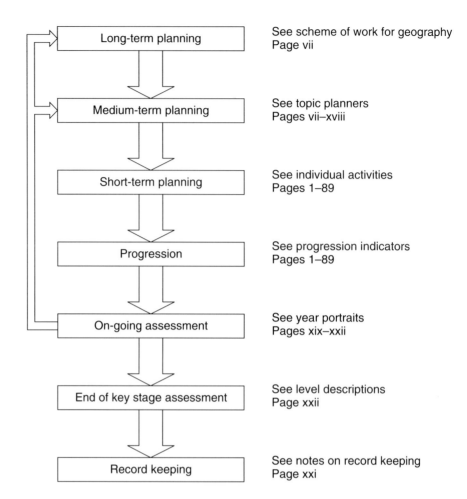

| | See scheme of work for geography
Page vii |
| Long-term planning | |

See topic planners
Pages vii–xviii

See individual activities
Pages 1–89

See progression indicators
Pages 1–89

See year portraits
Pages xix–xxii

See level descriptions
Page xxii

*Figure 3 How to plan
geographical activities*

See notes on record keeping
Page xxi

1. THE LOCAL AREA

By the time they come to school young children will already have acquired a certain amount of knowledge about the place where they live. This topic builds on and extends their experience. It considers houses, shops and jobs in the local area and provides opportunities for practical work in the school building and immediate surroundings. Links with other subjects include observing and naming building materials in science and finding out about historical sites.

Links to other subjects

Science
Name common materials
Plants and animals in the local environment.

History
Use buildings and sites to find out about the past.

Art
Work of artists, craftspeople and designers in the school locality.

Geography curriculum

Pupils should investigate the physical and human features of their surroundings. They should study the locality of the school which, at this key stage, consists of the school buildings and grounds and the surrounding area within easy access.

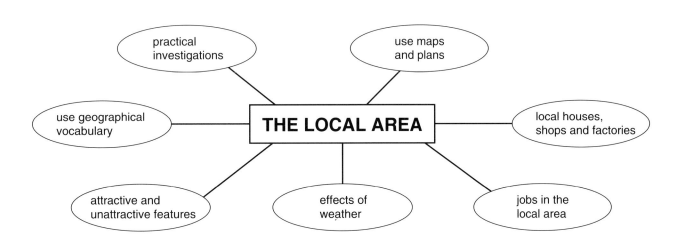

Activities

1. Our school	54. Class plan	93. Places snap
2. Classroom windows	55. Signpost map	94. Landmarks
3. Different views	56. Journey plan	96. Guide books
6. Our locality	58. Adventure playground	150. Types of house
7. The neighbourhood	61. Footprints	151. Your address
12. Classroom areas	62. Follow the route	163. Services in school
13. Areas in school	63. Tourist maps	171. School jobs
14. School walk	64. Journeys	179. Street work
15. School photo quiz	84. Rock collection	189. Journey to school
16. Familiar features	85. Investigating the school grounds	190. Transport survey
17. Fieldwork sketches	86. Different soils	203. Experiencing the weather
18. Street survey	87. Streets	204. All in a day
24. Familiar scenes	88. Street names	205. Recording the weather
25. Aerial photographs	89. Name rubbings	221. Water walk
44. Signs in school	90. Where we live	222. Playground quiz
45. School journeys	91. Picture map	226. Resources in the classroom
46. Signs in the street	92. Local goods and services	231. Made of iron and steel
47. Street trail		
48. Compass directions		

2. A CONTRASTING LOCALITY

One of the aims of the geography curriculum is to introduce children to the wider world. This topic focuses on a place which contrasts with the local area. If you choose somewhere that is only a short distance from your school you will be able to visit it with the children. However there are also good reasons for choosing distant places in order to extend the children's understanding. In either event the work should focus on daily life and include a balance of both physical and human geography.

Geography curriculum

> Pupils should be aware that the world extends beyond their own locality. They should study a contrasting locality either in the United Kingdom or overseas. The contrasting locality should be similar in size to the local area.

Links to other subjects

Science
Differences between local environments.

History
Way of life of people in Britain in the past.

Art
Art, craft and design from different places and times.

Music
Music from different times and cultures.

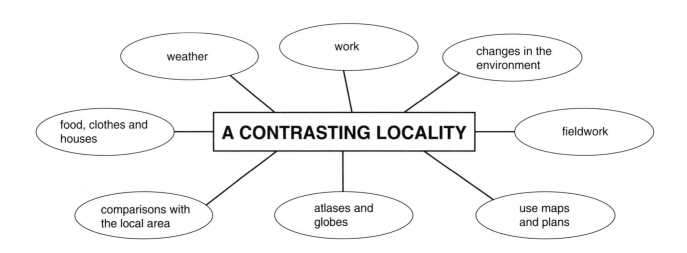

Activities
- 11. Looking at photographs
- 26. Postcards
- 27. Brochures
- 28. Map exhibition
- 29. Comparisons
- 31. Library quiz
- 32. Other countries
- 33. Stamps
- 50. North and South Pole
- 59. Adventure story
- 60. Treasure islands
- 67. Acrostic
- 68. The British Isles
- 69. Different countries
- 70. Countries snap
- 73. Connections
- 74. Impressions
- 75. Countries game
- 80. Capital cities
- 82. World map
- 83. Globe
- 98. Contrasts
- 99. Fishing port
- 100. Mining community
- 104. Food from different places
- 105. Holidays
- 106. Looking at pictures
- 107. Overseas communities
- 108. Travellers
- 109. Objects
- 110. Twinning
- 111. Buildings around the world
- 126. A far-away place
- 156. Concertina book
- 167. Markets
- 178. Jobs around the world
- 196. Obstacles
- 198. Holiday journeys
- 199. Adventure journeys
- 217. Clothes
- 218. World weather
- 224. Round the world

See also the studies of Broadwindsor and Sandwich, pp 41–43

3. THE ENVIRONMENT

This topic reflects the growing public interest and concern about our natural surroundings. It also harnesses more traditional geographical studies on natural resources and the way they are obtained. Children should be encouraged to express their views about the local environment. They also need to understand that places change and that they can be improved. This will help to channel the work in positive directions rather than dwelling on problems.

Geography curriculum

> The children should investigate the quality of the environment in any locality, either in the United Kingdom or overseas.

Links to other subjects

Science
Treat living things and the environment with care and sensitivity.

History
Changes in their own lives and those of their family.

Music
How sound is used to create particular effects, eg to soothe, to excite.

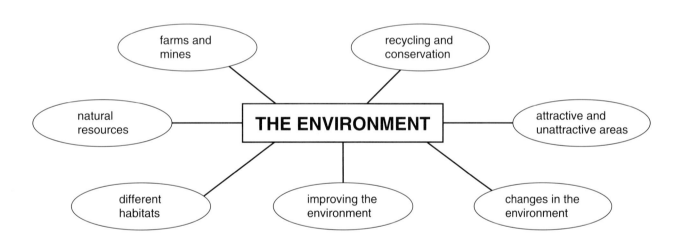

Activities

4. Teddy bear visit	131. Obsolete objects	146. Working for the environment
5. Personal feelings	132. New things	154. Front doors
118. Things we like in school	133. Door walk	158. Fantasy houses
119. Sensory walk	134. Advertisements	225. Natural resources
120. Word game	135. Favourite building	226. Resources in the classroom
121. The local environment	136. Wear and tear	227. Resources and products mobile
122. Different features	137. Classroom improvements	228. Wood rubbings
123. Different opinions	138. School improvements	229. Woollen clothes
124. Likes and dislikes	139. Dream ideas	231. Made of iron and steel
125. Good for children	140. Plans for the future	233. How are they obtained?
126. A far-away place	141. The outside view	235. Farming, fishing and mining
127. Things which change	142. Wildlife area	
128. Change dial	143. Tree planting	
129. Farms and factories	144. Recycling scheme	
130. Change in your local area	145. Improvements in the local area	

4. HOUSES

Young children quite naturally tend to see the world in terms of the things which are familiar in their daily lives, and teaching strategies which are based on this interest are likely to be particularly successful. 'Homes' is an ideal topic for drawing on personal experiences and involving children in simple fieldwork. It also provides plenty of opportunities for reinforcement.

If possible you should get the children to make drawings of houses in the local area and identify different buildings on a large scale plan. Photographs can help to enhance the work. You could ask the children to 'adopt' individual houses along a street and assemble the work as a class frieze. Investigations of structures and building materials provides another dimension.

Although much of the work will be based on the local area it also makes good sense to consider homes and houses in other places. This will illustrate how houses vary according to weather conditions and available materials. The links to other parts of the curriculum are also well worth pursuing and could involve paintings, poems and stories, perhaps through the theme of animal homes.

Geography curriculum

Pupils should be taught:

- to undertake fieldwork activities in the locality of the school, *eg observing housing types*
- how land and buildings, *eg farms, parks, factories, houses* are used.

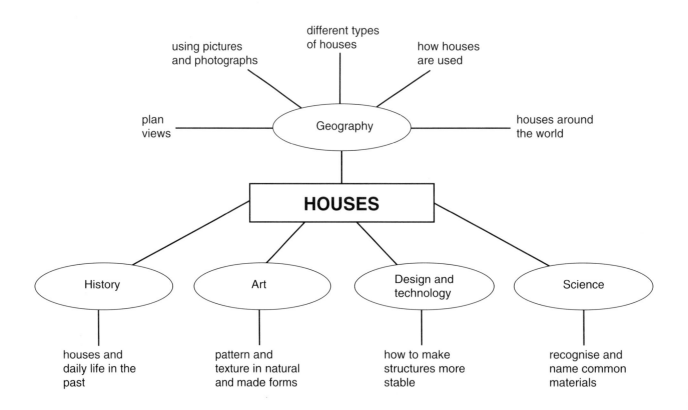

Activities

17. Fieldwork sketches	123. Different opinions	154. Front doors
18. Street survey	135. Favourite building	155. Streets and houses
24. Familiar scenes	142. Wildlife area	156. Concertina book
52. Plan views	147. Different buildings	157. House shapes
53. Tray games	148. Name the parts	158. Fantasy houses
54. Class plan	149. Rooms with a purpose	
90. Where we live	150. Types of house	See also the unit on visiting local
106. Looking at pictures	151. Your address	streets p 31
111. Buildings around the world	152. Animal addresses	
	153. House numbers	

5. SHOPS AND SERVICES

Most infants have direct experience of visiting the shops and buying things for themselves. They will also know about the different people who provide a service by helping behind the counter. This topic brings together these different ideas under a single heading and focuses attention on the immediate surroundings.

It is best not to take anything for granted. You need to discuss with the children what a shop actually is. Many children have a rather naive notion that shops are a kind of Aladdin's cave where you go to collect the things you want. It is useful to discuss why we give the shopkeeper money, where this money goes and where different products come from.

There is considerable potential for drama and role play. You could also consider product design in technology and how things work in science. Money and exercises based on coins provide a natural link to mathematics. The names of different shops and products introduce a linguistic dimension.

Geography curriculum

> Pupils should be taught about the main physical and human features *eg rivers, hills, factories and shops* that give the local area and a contrasting locality their character.

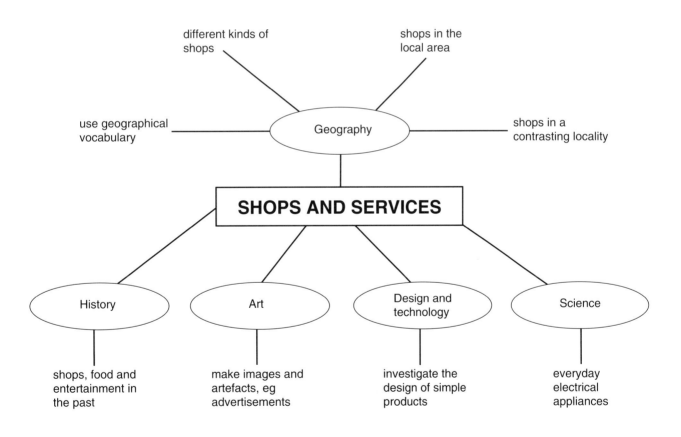

6. JOBS

The notion that work is purposeful activity is one that children take time to grasp. For many infants, life is a whole experience that is channelled by the occasional demands of adults. Play is a serious business, and events are not separated. A study of the different jobs done in a community and the roles that adults fulfil can enlarge the children's understanding and capture their imagination.

There are many questions to consider. What jobs do adults do in your school? What things are made locally? How do people get to work? Which jobs have to be done at night or at the weekends?

You may be able to introduce a practical element to the topic by visiting a farm, shop or some other place of work. Questionnaires will help the children collect information. Alternatively you might consider how goods are manufactured. The different stages in a production line make an interesting sequence. Young children often find it hard to associate products with raw materials. Further ideas are provided in the planner on Materials and Resources.

Geography curriculum

Pupils should be taught about the main physical and human features, *eg rivers, hills, factories, shops* that give localities their character.

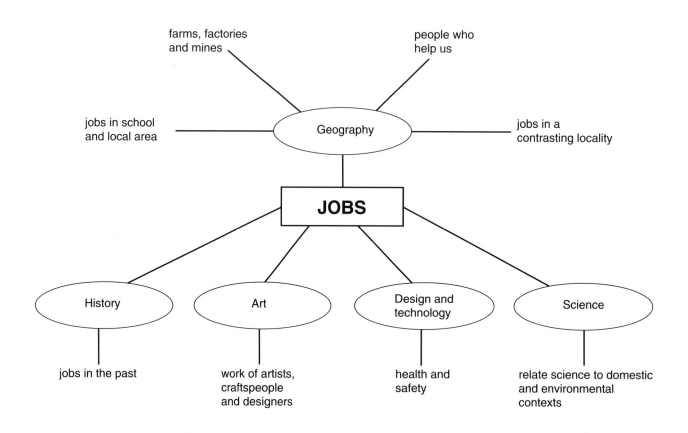

Activities
21. Making things
99. Fishing port
100. Mining community
106. Looking at pictures
129. Farms and factories
146. Working for the environment
170. What is work?
171. School jobs
172. Job fact files
173. Music while you work
174. Running a school
175. People who help us
176. Places of work
177. A dictionary of jobs
178. Jobs around the world
179. Street work
180. Tools and equipment
181. Acting a job
182. Car production line
183. A place of work

See also the unit on Broadwindsor, pp 41–42

7. JOURNEYS

'Journeys' is a popular topic at Key Stage One. There is little doubt that children enjoy finding out about distant places and how to reach them. They are often fascinated by different vehicles and methods of transport and enjoy looking at the machines and equipment. The idea of travel provides a focus for many children's books and provides a natural way of extending the work.

There are many questions to investigate. Why do people travel? What routes do they take? How does the driver know which way to go? How have vehicles changed? As well as finding out the answers to these questions from direct observation, the children may also want to consult information books and other secondary sources.

The links with other areas of the curriculum are also easy to develop. Movement and forces are key ideas in science, the design of vehicles introduces technology, while changes in transport leads back into history. From a geographical point of view any work on a contrasting locality will involve questions about links and journeys from the local area. This means you can introduce the work in a number of different ways.

Geography curriculum

Pupils should be taught to:

- follow directions, including the terms up, down, on, under, behind, in front of, near, far, left, right, north, south, east, west;
- make maps and plans, *eg a plan of their route from home to school.*

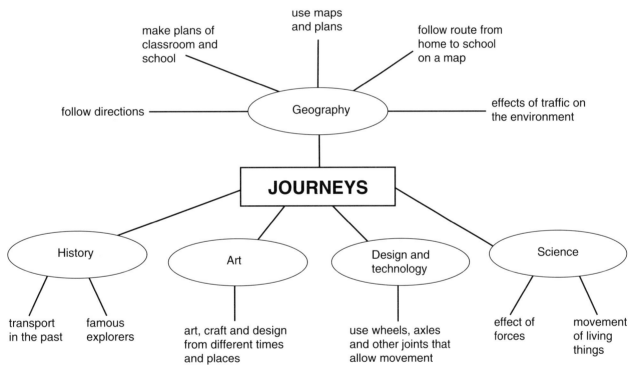

Activities

14. School walk	62. Follow the route	191. Vehicle collage
23. Roads	63. Tourist maps	192. Bus journeys
38. Left and right	64. Journeys	193. Deliveries
39. Left and right stick	65. On the road	194. Places to visit
40. Left and right survey	83. Globe	195. Direction signs
41. Direction finder	184. Journeys around the school	196. Obstacles
42. Mystery trail	185. Reasons for travel	197. Toy vehicles
43. Programmable toy	186. Journey survey	198. Holiday journeys
44. Signs in school	187. Ways of travelling	199. Adventure journeys
45. School journeys	188. Near or far?	200. Stories of journeys
55. Signpost map	189. Journey to school	
56. Journey plan	190. Transport survey	See also the unit on visiting a bus station, p 34
61. Footprints		

8. WEATHER

The weather influences our daily lives and, over longer periods, provides a pattern to the year. Many infant teachers will be familiar with this topic which has been a favourite for many years. The web diagram illustrates the potential for work across the curriculum.

In geography, children should record the weather over a short period of time and make their own observations. They should also consider the difference between the seasons and make comparisons with other places around the world. Finally, they might discuss the way in which weather affects plants and animals.

For historical studies there are many pictures, stories and poems which describe how life followed the seasons in the past. There is a vivid and valuable link to geography through historic natural disasters including Noah's flood. In science the effect of light on plants, the differences between day and night and the way temperature affects materials provide a range of different approaches. Paintings and pictures of the weather can be used to introduce a more subjective approach.

Geography curriculum

Pupils should be taught about the effects of weather on people and their surroundings, *eg the effect of seasonal variations in temperature on the clothes people wear.*

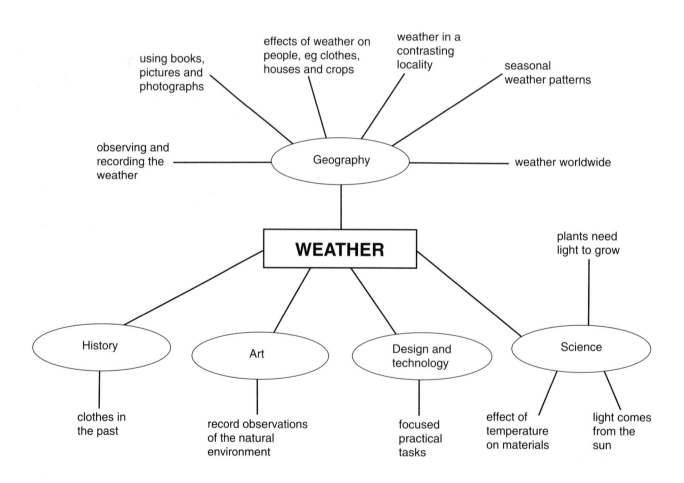

Activities

10. Word scales	206. Weather dial	213. Seasonal words
113. Soft toys	207. Weather forecast	214. Poetry box
201. Weather words	208. The right weather	215. Seasonal cluedo
202. Weather symbols	209. Wind testers	216. Dressed for the season
203. Experiencing the weather	210. Weather picture	217. Clothes
204. All in a day	211. Weather music	218. World weather
205. Recording the weather	212. Season tree	

9. WATER

'Water' is a popular topic at Key Stage 1. It has the advantage of building on and extending children's natural interest in the environment and it covers a wide variety of themes. However, an all-embracing topic of this kind runs the risk of becoming over-general. There is much to be said for taking a particular angle or perspective.

Any project on water will provide plenty of opportunities for fieldwork. The children could consider how we use water in our daily lives, they could look for ways in which water enters and leaves the school building and they could find out about local ponds, streams and rivers. If you live near the sea, then you could make a visit to the beach. Work on seas and oceans could also be pursued through maps, books and other secondary sources.

The cross-curricular links are equally varied. They include the effect of water on people and plants in science, the way we use water in cooking in technology classes and studies of the natural environment in art. You might also refer to the topic planner on 'journeys' to explore how water both creates obstacles but can also be used as a means of communication.

Geography curriculum

> Pupils should be taught about the main physical and human features, *eg rivers* that give the localities their character.

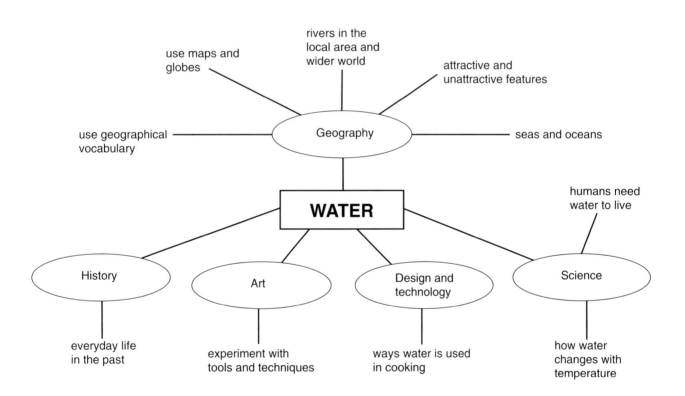

Activities

26. Postcards
29. Comparisons
30. Picture viewer
31. Library quiz
59. Adventure story
60. Treasure islands

103. Postcard corner
196. Obstacles
199. Adventure journeys
219. Water experiments
220. Word mobile
221. Water walk

222. Playground quiz
223. Water and landscapes
224. Round the world
239. Fish mobile

10. MATERIALS AND RESOURCES

This topic considers different natural resources, the way they are obtained and how they are used. Young children often find it hard to associate materials and products so they will need to spend time making links and connections. Even adults sometimes find it hard to recognise that plastics, wax, petrol and gas all come from oil. Similarly, infants are often bemused that paper comes from wood and that glass is made from sand.

The way that raw materials are obtained is often a subject of considerable interest. Coal comes from mines under the ground, stone and gravel from quarries and leather from cattle. Children often enjoy finding out about the processes of production. There may be opportunities for a farm visit which will help to provide a practical dimension.

Another approach is to consider the materials themselves. How many can the children identify and name? You might set up an interest table and encourage the class to contribute different examples. The links with other topics, particularly homes and houses, is one that you might decide to develop as appropriate.

Geography curriculum

> Pupils should be taught about the main physical and human features that give the localities their character.

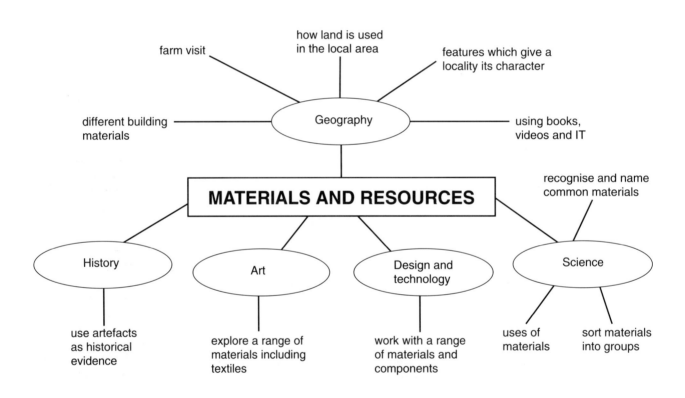

Activities
144. Recycling scheme
225. Natural resources
226. Resources in the classroom
227. Resources and products mobile
228. Wood rubbings
229. Woollen clothes

230. Miniature characters
231. Made of iron and steel
232. Zig-zag book
233. How are they obtained?
234. Different sources
235. Farming, fishing and mining.
236. Machines

237. Underground scene
238. Fishing fleet
239. Fish mobile

See also the units on Visiting a Church, p 32, and Visiting a Farm, p 36

PROGRESSION AND ASSESSMENT

Schools need to devise a system for tracking pupils' progress through each Key Stage. Under the current regulations parents can expect to receive an annual report describing the range and quality of their child's work in geography. Feedback is also essential for your own short- and medium-term planning.

Progression

The programme of study for geography is divided into a number of different elements within the overall structure of skills, places and themes. The way in which these represent a basis for describing progression and achievement is shown in Figure 1.

Year portraits

If you want to assess children's work continuously throughout the school year you will find it helpful to use the progression indicators given at the beginning of each of the units in this book. Alternatively you might decide to assess your pupils in a more general way. The following portraits indicate what a typical child might be expected to achieve by the end of each school year. As well as providing a description, the portraits also include references to teaching activities and copymasters. These can be used to support the work and as evidence of achievements.

	SKILLS		PLACES AND THEMES		
	Asking questions	*Using skills*	*Places*	*Processes*	*Environment*
Reception	Answer questions about their immediate surroundings	Find their way round the classroom using simple directional terms	Talk about different places described in stories and fairy tales	Name some key features of the local area	Talk about safe and dangerous places
Year 1	Ask simple questions about their immediate surroundings	Draw plan views of everyday objects	Know about some of the different environments around the world	Recognise that features can be sorted into groups	Talk about attractive and unattractive places
Year 2	Discuss different questions to investigate	Show the sequence of events in a story or along a route	Name continents and oceans on a globe or atlas map	Distinguish between physical and human features	Describe how places can be changed or improved

Figure 1 Summary of typical progress through Key Stage 1. Individual children may be above or below these general indicators.

Reception

Much of the work with children of this age will involve observing and talking.

Geographical skills

The children should be able to recognise different parts of the classroom and find their way round using simple directional words such as up, down, in front of and behind. They should be able to draw a picture of what they have seen on a short walk or the events in a story with a geographical focus.

Places and themes

The children should be able to talk about their experiences in different places and in different types of weather. They will be able to recognise safe and dangerous places and be able to name some of the main features in the local environment such as hills, streams, shops, churches and parks.

	Activities		Copymasters	
Geographical skills	2.	Classroom windows	1.	Window view
	4.	Teddy bear visit	6.	In the street
	16.	Familiar features	15.	Street signs
	26.	Postcards	22.	Tracks
	34.	Direction words	29.	Flags (1)
	38.	Left and right	30.	Flags (2)
	46.	Signs in the street		
	61.	Footprints		
	71.	Different flags		
Places and themes	119.	Sensory walk	42.	At the park I-spy
	125.	Good for children	61.	Smells I don't like
	201.	Weather words	62.	Sounds I don't like
	216.	Dressed for the season	63.	Things I like to touch
	221.	Water walk	108.	The right clothes
	228.	Wood rubbings	112.	Water survey
			116.	Trees are wood

Year 1

Much of the work with children of this age will involve naming and using vocabulary.

Geographical skills

The children should be able to follow directions round the classroom and school building. They should know that objects look different when viewed from different angles, and be able to draw simple plan views. They will be able to recognise the shape of the British Isles on a map.

Places and themes

The children will begin to recognise that there are different types of shops and houses in the local area. They will be able to talk about changes in the school building and local area. They will know that there are other places and environments around the world which provide a habitat for plants and creatures.

	Activities		Copymasters	
Geographical skills	18.	Street survey	7.	Street survey
	28.	Map exhibition	11.	Which country?
	51.	Overhead projector	18.	Plan views
	52.	Plan views	28.	Different shapes
	55.	Signpost map	31.	UK jigsaw
	70.	Countries snap		
	77.	Jigsaw puzzle		
Places and themes	87.	Streets	38.	Street walk
	113.	Soft toys	40.	Going shopping
	121.	The local environment	65.	Different environments
	127.	Things which change	66.	Things which change
	181.	Acting a job	90.	Different hats
	202.	Weather symbols	103.	Weather snap

Year 2

Much of the work with children of this age will involve grouping and sorting.

Geographical skills

The children should be able to draw a pictorial map to show their route from home to school, marking the landmarks in the correct order. They will have used large-scale maps and aerial photographs of the local area. They will be able to name the continents and oceans on an atlas map or globe.

Places and themes

The children will be able to make simple comparisons between their own area and a contrasting locality. They will know that places change and that pollution affects the environment in a number of ways. They will be able to talk about attractive and unattractive places, discuss how places can be improved and obtain information from books and other secondary sources with guidance.

	Activities	Copymasters
Geographical skills	6. Our locality 9. Landscapes 10. Word scales 14. School walk 32. Other countries 48. Compass directions 56. Journey plan 82. World map	3. Landscapes 5. School walk 12. Features 16. Compass directions 19. Route maze
Places and themes	90. Where we live 96. Guide book 103. Postcard corner 109. Objects 138. School improvements 141. The outside view 150. Types of house 156. Concertina book 189. Journey to school	34. Where I live 70. School improvements 71. Different views 76. House model 81. Houses worldwide 96. Journey to school See also sheets 50–57 on Broadwindsor and Sandwich

Record keeping

Any records you decide to keep need to be manageable to maintain and easy to consult. They also have to provide meaningful information about the progress which the child is making. The sample sheet shown in Figure 2 is one way of tracking pupils' progress. On this system, pupils who are consistently satisfactory or above average at the end of year 2 are likely to match the national curriculum level descriptions for level 2 or 3. Pupils who need help will probably fit the descriptions for levels 1 or 2.

School ....

Pupil ....

Subject ....

Record pupils' progress using these symbols

A: Above average
S: Satisfactory
H: Needs help to make progress

Year	Project	Skills	Places and Themes
R			
	End of year summary		
1			
	End of year summary		
2			
	End of year summary		

Level at the end of KS1 (please circle)   1   2   3

Figure 2 Sample record sheet for tracking pupils' progress.

End of Key Stage Assessment

Level descriptions have been included in the national curriculum so teachers can assess children's progress and achievement at the end of each key stage. SCAA has given clear instructions that the level descriptions should not be broken down into a set of 'mini' statements or tick lists as this will take an unreasonable amount of time and lead to fragmentation of the curriculum. Instead, teachers should use the descriptions to make rounded judgements about the child's overall performance. SCAA also recognises that children are often more advanced in one aspect of a subject than another so there is little point in looking for an exact fit between pupils' work and the level descriptions. What is required is a more holistic approach which considers the overall quality of the child's learning.

Level Descriptions for Key Stage 1

Level 1

Pupils recognise and make observations about physical and human features of places. They express their views on features of the environment of a locality that they find attractive or unattractive. They use resources provided and their own observations to respond to questions about places.

Level 2

Pupils describe physical and human features of places, recognising those features that give places their character. They show an awareness of places beyond their own locality. They express views on attractive and unattractive features of the environment of a locality. Pupils select information from resources provided. They use this information and their own observations to ask and respond to questions about places. They begin to use appropriate vocabulary.

Level 3

Pupils describe and make comparisons between the physical and human features of different localities. They offer explanations for the locations of some of those features. They show an awareness that different places may have both similar and different characteristics. They offer reasons for some of their observations and judgements about places. They use skills and sources of evidence to respond to a range of geographical questions.

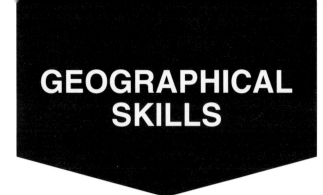

GEOGRAPHICAL SKILLS

■ **2.** In investigating places and a theme, pupils should be given opportunities to observe, question and record, and to communicate ideas and information.

■ **3.** Pupils should be taught to:

a use geographical terms, *eg hill, river, road,* in exploring their surroundings;

b undertake fieldwork activities in the locality of the school, *eg observing housing types, mapping the school playground;*

c follow directions, including the terms up, down, on, under, behind, in front of, near, far, left, right, north, south, east, west;

d make maps and plans of real and imaginary places, using pictures and symbols, *eg a pictorial map of a place featured in a story, a plan of their route from home to school;*

e use globes, maps and plans at a variety of scales; the work should include identifying major geographical features, *eg seas, rivers, cities,* locating and naming on a map the constituent countries of the United Kingdom, marking on a map approximately where they live, and following a route;

f use secondary sources, *eg pictures, photographs (including aerial photographs),* books, videos, CD-ROM encyclopaedia, to obtain geographical information.

Geographers seek to describe the world. In order to do this they have pioneered a number of special skills and techniques. Fieldwork enables geographers to collect information and data about conditions in different places. This information can then be analysed using maps.

This chapter highlights geographical skills. For ease of reference fieldwork and research are considered first and mapwork second. Although the activities concentrate on geography, the opportunities for cross-curricular work will be immediately apparent.

Mapreading involves the use of co-ordinates, directions and geometrical shapes. Fieldwork develops the use of vocabulary and simple sketching techniques while research requires a basic level of literacy and the ability to analyse information.

FIELDWORK AND RESEARCH

All geographical work done outside the classroom is known as fieldwork. With infants the main focus will be on sensory perception, vocabulary and simple data collection. If children are to have a chance to develop skills in these areas they will need to undertake fieldwork on a regular basis. Over a period of time this will enable them to build up an increasingly sophisticated image of their immediate surroundings.

As they conduct their studies, children should be encouraged to ask questions about the world around them. As well as naming physical and human features in the local environment you might encourage them to speculate about what different places are like and how they came to be as they are. Just as scientists undertake tests and experiments to find out about the properties of different materials, so geographers need to collect information at first hand. Trails, surveys and questionnaires all have a part to play. On occasions you may also want to use specialist equipment such as a tape measure or magnetic compass.

All fieldwork needs to be carefully planned. If you have clear aims and objectives and give the children focused tasks, you are likely to achieve the best results.

You also need to sort out the organisational details. It is essential to explore the area beforehand. You need to prepare your helpers, explain what you want to achieve and see that you have a good adult : pupil ratio. You will of course have to obtain permission from parents beforehand and follow any safety procedures laid down by the school.

Outings do not necessarily have to be lengthy. Nor do they need to focus on places that are remarkable or unusual. Some of the best work is done in local roads and side streets as HMI reports affirm. What matters most is that there is a clear structure and the children know what they are doing and that it is within their ability.

When you return to school you should follow up the work by getting the children to think about what they have discovered. You may also want to extend the work through research using secondary sources. The geography Order specifically mentions pictures, photographs, books, videos and CD-ROM encyclopaedias. You might also arrange for talks from visitors. In this way the children will deepen their understanding and gain a better understanding of geographical concepts.

USE GEOGRAPHICAL VOCABULARY ▶

Pupils should be taught to use geographical terms, *eg hill, river, road*, in exploring their surroundings.

Progression indicators
- name key features on a walk or trail
- recognise that geographical features can be sorted into groups
- describe the local area in geographical terms

Interpretation
The children should talk about their immediate surroundings and consider physical, human and environmental aspects of their home school and neighbourhood.

Introduction
The relationship between thought and language is highly complex. However, unless children have appropriate vocabulary, it is unlikely they will be able to develop their ideas. This unit draws attention to the role of language in promoting learning.

Like any subject, geography has its own specialist terminology. At infant level many of these terms are part of everyday speech. This reflects the fact that geographers describe the world around us. When identifying the words that young children need to know it is often helpful to think in terms of categories or groups. For this reason the list of key vocabulary below is listed under headings.

You need to remember that children need a lot of practice in using new vocabulary before they fully understand its use. Children often guess what to do when the whole class is given instructions, and it only becomes clear that they have not understood what to do when they are asked to work on their own. Constant reinforcement and the opportunity to use vocabulary in different ways will help children to develop their ability to recall geographical terms.

Key vocabulary

Landscape

bank	hill	sea
cliff	mountain	stream
field	river	wood

Buildings and places

church	house	playground
factory	office	school
garage	park	shop

Routes

alley	motorway	street
bypass	railway	subway
footpath	road	track

Boundaries

barrier	fence	kerb
bridge	gate	shore
edge	hedge	wall

Weather

breeze	fog	rain
cloud	frost	shower
cold	gale	storm
dry	hot	thunder
flood	ice	wind

Environmental quality

attractive	litter	quiet
beautiful	noisy	smelly
interesting	pollution	smokey

Key questions

What words describe the landscape and other physical features?
What words describe buildings and places?
What words describe the environment?

Resources

Songs

The children may enjoy 'Tipsy Topsy Turvy Town' from *The Music Box Songbook* (BBC, 1987) as it is full of simple absurdities.

Picture books

Many picture books use geographical vocabulary as a natural part of the story. *We're Going on a Bear Hunt* by Michael Rosen and Helen Oxenbury (Walker, 1989) is a good example. The search in the story leads to lots of different places including a cave and a forest. *Anno's Journey* by Mitsumasa Anno (Bodley, 1977) adopts a different format but also helps to stimulate vocabulary. It is a picture book without words that takes the reader on a journey across the landscapes of Europe.

Activity 1 Our school

Materials needed

Large sheets of paper and artwork materials.

Talk with the class about the school. How many classrooms are there? How many teachers? What are the walls made of? How many different entrances are there? Is the building all on the same floor or level? Ask the children to make paintings of the school, showing the things which they think are important. Put these up as a class display and add notes highlighting the main features shown.

Activity 2 Classroom windows

Materials needed

Fabric, coloured paper and other materials for a collage.

Discuss with the children what they can see through one of the classroom windows. Can they identify houses, trees, churches, shops, fields, hedges, hills, clouds, and

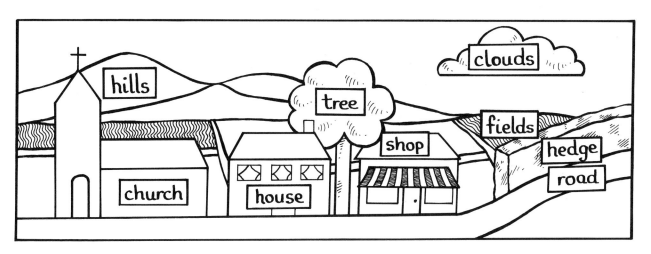

so on? Put out some fabric, coloured paper and other materials and ask the children to make a collage of the view. Mount the collages on the wall and add labels naming the key features. Use **Copymaster 1** (Window View) as a way of extending the work.

Activity 3 Different views

Compare the view from four or five different windows around the school. Which window has the most interesting view? From which window can you see most things? Which windows has your favourite view? Get the children to vote on the view they like most. Make up some sentences to record the children's opinions, for example, 'Seven children like the view from the hall window'. 'You can see five different buildings from the windows in Class 1'.

Activity 4 Teddy bear visit

Materials needed

Teddy Bears, camera and film, scrapbook.

Arrange for the children to bring their teddy bears to school for the day. (Make sure that bears are provided for any children who don't have their own bear.) Talk with the children about the places and things they should show their bears. Where can they play? Where can they go for a drink? Where do they work? Take photographs of the bears in these different places and mount them in a book called 'Teddy Comes to School'. The children should write a sentence under each photograph. With more mature children you might also include a simple map at the beginning showing the places visited.

Activity 5 Personal feelings

Materials needed

Large-scale plan of the school.

Make a collection of words which describe what we feel about different places. Examples could include 'interesting', 'quiet', 'noisy', 'exciting', 'colourful', 'frightening', and so on. Visit some places around the school and get the children to say which words best describe their feelings. When they return to the class

> I like the playground because it is noisy.
> John

ask the children to write some simple sentences about what they felt. You could pin these to a large-scale map of the school to make a wall display. Are there any places which some children like but which others dislike? Which places do the children generally like to visit?

Activity 6 Our locality

Materials needed

Large-scale map of the locality, computer and database program.

Working as a class or in groups, discuss all the different places and buildings you can think of in your locality. You may find it helpful to look at a large-scale map of the locality. Make a list of facts and figures. How many churches are there? How many shops? How many streets? Is there a park? If possible, enter these facts and figures into a simple computer database and print out the statistics.

Activity 7 The neighbourhood

Materials needed

Old shoe boxes or cardboard boxes.

Talk with the children about the school and its neighbourhood. What different buildings are there? What routes do people use? Are there any special places, such as a park or old castle? Choose three or four key places and get the children to bring items from them to school for display. For example, they might bring old tickets, pictures, timetables and brochures from the bus station. Make a box for each place. You could put labels and photographs on the front and set them up as a small exhibition.

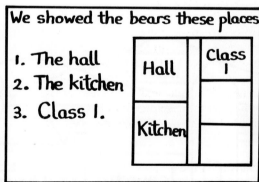

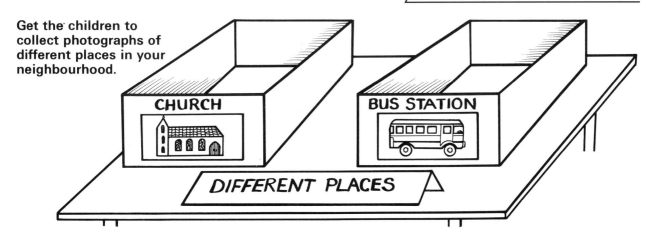

Get the children to collect photographs of different places in your neighbourhood.

Activity 8: Jigsaw scenes

Materials needed

A selection of simple jigsaws.

Give the children some simple jigsaws to complete, showing town or country scenes. Talk with them about the different things in the picture. Ask them to make a list of appropriate words using geographical headings such as 'buildings', 'transport' or 'scenery'. You could extend the work by giving the class **Copymaster 2** (Jigsaw). The children should colour the picture and talk about the different features they can see. They could then cut up the pieces and try to put them together in the correct order. Alternatively, you could play a game of beetle, in which the children throw a dice to see which pieces they collect. The winner is the first person to make up a complete scene.

Activity 9 Landscapes

Materials needed

Frieze paper, scissors, glue.

Get the children to colour **Copymaster 3** (Landscapes), and cut out the pictures. They should then try to arrange them in a logical order, from the peak to the sea. Check that the children have put the pictures in a sensible sequence and get them to glue them down on a piece of frieze paper. Finally, display the work on the classroom wall and discuss any differences that you notice. Although there is an overall pattern, the children may have decided to put the wood and field in a variety of different positions.

Activity 10 Word scales

Get the children to make a list of all the words they can think of which describe different types of wind. Put them down in random order and then try to sort them into a sequence. For example, you might start with 'calm' and 'light breeze' at one end of the scale and conclude with 'gale' and 'hurricane' at the other. Ask the children to make drawings to go with some of the words. Put them up with captions as a class display.

CALM
Smoke rises upwards

BREEZE
Kites fly

WINDY
Waves at sea

GALE
Trees blow over

Think about some other word scales. For example, there are lots of different words that describe temperature, or settlements (hamlets, villages, towns and so on), or types of transport.

Activity 11 Looking at photographs

Materials needed

Photographs of scenes from around the world.

Give the children some pictures to look at showing scenes from around the world. Discuss what they show. Get the children to select two which they find particularly interesting and to record information about them using **Copymaster 4** (Looking at Photographs). Extend the work by showing the class some slides of different places. What are the key features in each picture? Can the children guess the country or continent?

Blueprints links

Many of the sheets in the *Infant Geography Resource Bank* develop geographical terms. See especially sheet 10 'Types of House', sheet 82 'Where we find Water' and sheet 104 'Hills'.

LOCAL FIELDWORK

Pupils should be taught to undertake fieldwork activities in the locality of the school, *eg observing housing types, mapping the school playground.*

Progression indicators
- record information on a tick sheet
- make simple drawings of local environmental features
- draw plans of the local area

Interpretation
The children should collect information about their classroom and school building, go on environmental walks in the local area and find out about different aspects of the place where they live.

Introduction
Children often learn best when they collect information for themselves and seek out the answer to different questions. This unit emphasises the importance of using the local area as a source of information in geography.

Most children will benefit from making studies in the classroom and school building before they tackle outdoor work. When they have acquired appropriate vocabulary and have developed a concept of area, they will then be able to look at local streets and buildings. It may also be possible to set up simple investigations for the children to work on.

Key vocabulary
bank	park
building	path
car park	place
church	post office
classroom	road
factory	school
house	shop
newsagent	street

Key questions
What are the different buildings and places in the local area?

How are they used?
What are the features which give our area its character?

Resources

Rhymes
This Little Puffin by Elizabeth Mattersen (Puffin, 1969) is full of ideas about the child's everyday world and environment.

Songs
You will need to choose any songs to match the environment around your school. For those who live in urban areas 'Sing a Song of People' and 'Tower Block' from *Songs from Play School* (Black, 1967) are particularly relevant.

Activity 12 Classroom areas

Materials needed
Large-scale plan of the classroom, labels, drawing pins.

Make a large-scale plan of the classroom and pin it on to the wall. Talk about the plan with the children. Can they identify the doors and windows? Where is their table or desk? Give the children labels describing how different areas are used. For example, one label might say 'This space is used for painting', and another might say 'This is where we keep our books'. Ask the children to pin the

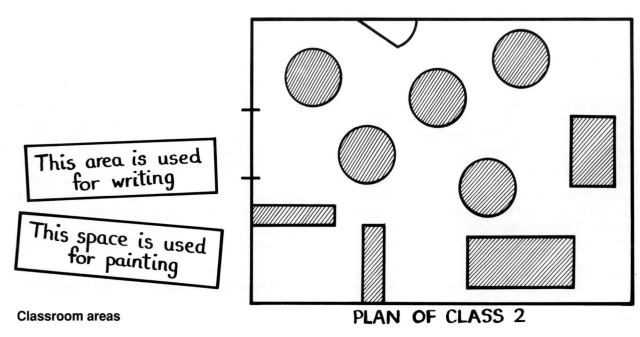

Classroom areas

PLAN OF CLASS 2

labels on to the correct part of the plan. Which things seem to take up the most space? Which things only need a small area? Are there any surprises or unexpected conclusions?

Activity 13 Areas in school

Materials needed
Large-scale plan of the school, labels, drawing pins.

Working in groups, go on a short walk around your school. Visit a number of different places. Ask the children what they are used for. Make a master list when you return to the classroom and get the children to pin labels on to a plan in the same way as they did for Activity 12.

Activity 14 School walk

Materials needed
Clipboards, paper.

Plan a walk around the school to visit all the different areas. Equip the children with clipboards, paper and pencils. As they go round they should note down how each place is used on a simple data collection sheet (see opposite page). Alternatively, you could get them to count up the number of different areas using **Copymaster 5** (School Walk).

PLACE	WHAT IS IT USED FOR?
Staffroom	Teachers relax here
Corridor	People walk along here

Activity 15 School photo quiz

Materials needed
Camera and film.

Take some photographs of different features of the school building such as doors, windows and decorations. Give the photographs to a group of children and see if they can find the things shown. You might need to sort the photographs into groups or give the children clues as to where to search if they get stuck. When the children have finished the quiz you could ask them to make pencil drawings of the things shown in the pictures and mount them with captions as a wall display.

Activity 16 Familiar features

Materials needed
Photographs of features in the vicinity of the school.

Talk with the children about familiar features in the vicinity of the school. What are the things they notice? What makes them special? Ask the children to make drawings of some of them. It is helpful to have a collection of photographs of local features to refer to. You could prepare this collection beforehand, or you could take the pictures during an environmental walk with the class. Use **Copymaster 6** (In the Street) to extend the work. This is designed to reinforce basic vocabulary.

Activity 17 Fieldwork sketches

Materials needed
Clipboards, pencils, paper, class scrapbook.

Arrange visits to a number of local streets and buildings. Ask the children to make simple field sketches of things that interest them. These could be small details such as door knockers and letter boxes, as well as more general scenes. When you return to school get the children to write a description to go with each drawing and put their work in a class scrapbook. What are the features that identify different streets?

Activity 18 Street survey

Materials needed
Ordnance Survey map of the locality.

Arrange a visit to a street near your school. Try to choose somewhere with a variety of buildings and give the children **Copymaster 7** (Street Survey) to help them record what they find. Back at school you could make a block graph showing the buildings in the street you visited. You might also look at a large-scale Ordnance Survey map. Can the children find the key buildings, such as the shops and the church? How many houses can they see? How can you tell the difference between buildings by looking at their plan?

Activity 19 Different places

Materials needed
Camera and film, card labels.

Take a number of photographs of buildings and places in the vicinity of the school. Make a pair of labels to go with each photograph. The first label should describe the place, the second label should indicate how it is used. For example, a picture of the local church would need a label giving its name and a label saying 'prayers, weddings, and other church services'. Ask the children to match the photographs with the labels. It may help if you use different-coloured card for the different types of label. You can reinforce this work with **Copymaster 8** (Different Places), in which children link places with the way they are used.

Activity 20 Selling things

Talk with the children about the different places you can go to buy things in the immediate neighbourhood. Can they name some of the shops? What are the things they

Different places. Take photographs of different buildings and places.

Photographs ⟶

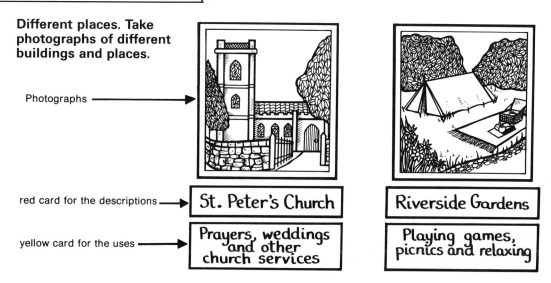

red card for the descriptions ⟶ St. Peter's Church

yellow card for the uses ⟶ Prayers, weddings and other church services

Riverside Gardens

Playing games, picnics and relaxing

can buy there? Make a visit to a local shopping precinct or shopping street. Collect information about the different shops using **Copymaster 9** (Shop Survey). Discuss the findings with the children when you return to school. Are there any shops which you would like to see set up in the area? Are any shops closing down? Can the children think of any changes to the shops?

Activity 21 Making things

Materials needed
Large-scale Ordnance Survey map of the local area, clipboards, pencils, paper.

Are there any places near your school where goods are made? Do any of the children have parents who work in local factories? What do they do? Look at a large-scale Ordnance Survey map of your area. Can the children identify the different places of work? Arrange a walk to visit some of them, and ask the children to make sketches to show what they look like.

Activity 22 Games and pastimes

Materials needed
General artwork materials.

Discuss the different places where the children go to play. Where are the nearest play areas, parks and sports centres? Are there any pieces of open ground which the children use unofficially? Ask the children to make a painting of a place where they play for a wall display. Get them to write a description underneath saying where it is, how it is used and whether the facilities are adequate (for example, 'There are lots of swings'.)

Activity 23 Roads

Materials needed
Large-scale Ordnance Survey map of the local area, camera and film.

Nearly a third of the land in towns and cities is taken up by roads and car parks. How many can you find on an Ordnance Survey map of your area? Working with the children, make a list of alleyways, cul-de-sacs, streets, paths, cycle tracks and dual carriageways near your school. Plan a walk that links together a range of different examples. Visit them with the children and take photographs to show what they look like for a class display.

Blueprints links
See sheet 81 'Transport', sheet 91 'Make a weather record' and sheet 92 'The Weather Chart' in the *Infant Geography Resource Bank*.

USE SECONDARY SOURCES ▶

Pupils should be taught to use secondary sources, *eg pictures, photographs including aerial photographs, books, videos, CD-ROM, encyclopaedias*, to obtain geographical information.

Progression indicators
• name features in photographs, postcards and other images of distant places
• find appropriate sections in simple reference books
• make simple comparisons between the local area and other places

Interpretation
The children should use a range of resources to find out about the local area, other places in the UK and the wider world.

Introduction

The previous unit concentrates on fieldwork and shows how children can study the local environment. This unit extends and develops the work by illustrating the value of secondary sources. These will be especially relevant for the study of distant places which the children are unable to visit for themselves.

There is a wide range of resources from which to choose. This includes:

- postcards
- photographs
- maps
- brochures
- newspapers
- posters
- magazines
- information books
- story books
- videos
- stamps, coins and artefacts
- encyclopaedias
- computer datafiles

Young children often find it hard to use secondary sources. Simple enquiry questions such as 'What is this place like?' and 'What would it be like to live here'? can help to focus their attention. Visual images will be particularly useful as many infants are unable to read much text. Again it is best to structure their enquiries. You could ask them to look up information about clothing, housing, weather, vegetation, landscape and other geographical themes. As the children become more skilled at looking for clues, photographs and postcards are likely to be a major teaching resource. If you can build up your own reference bank this will be an extra asset.

Key vocabulary

bridge	home	river
city	lake	street
factory	marsh	town
farm	motorway	valley
field	mountain	village
forest	place	weather
hill	railway	wood

Key questions

What are the main landscape features?
Are there any roads and buildings?
What do you think the weather is like?
Would you like to live in this place?

Resources

Picture books

Gerry's Seaside Journey by Michelle Cartlidge (Heinemann, 1988) is an enchanting story of a family of teddy bears that moves to the seaside. The pictures and text describe a number of different places, such as city streets, the motorway, a garage and country lanes.

Songs

'A Windmill in Old Amsterdam', from *Apusskidu* by Beatrice Harrop (Black, 1975) is a popular song which helps to provide the children with an image of another part of the world.

Teaching packs

The *World Watch Geography Themes Pack* (Collins, 1993) contains 48 laminated A3 photographs for children to discuss and use as reference sources. The photographs are arranged into themes such as houses, transport, weather and conservation.

Activity 24 Familiar scenes

Materials needed
Camera and film.

Take some photographs of different features of the local area. Try to include some physical features, such as hills, as well as streets and buildings. Make a display of the photographs and see if the children can recognise them. Ask them to write a sentence saying what each one shows. Encourage them to find out more about each photograph by asking geographical questions. **Copymaster 10** (Photograph Survey) will help to structure the work.

Activity 25 Aerial photographs

Materials needed
Aerial photographs of the school or local area.

Show the children an aerial photograph of the school building or local area. Talk about the different features you can see and get them to make a list. What else can the children learn from the photograph? For example, are there any clues which indicate the time of day or season of the year? Have there been any changes since the picture was taken? Think about the different zones and areas which are shown. Can the children use the photograph to find a route which they know, eg round the school grounds or along local streets?

Activity 26 Postcards

Materials needed
Postcards, old shoe boxes.

Make a collection of postcards of different places in the United Kingdom and abroad. You could start the collection off with some postcards of your own, but the children should also be invited to contribute. Put out some old shoe boxes so that the children can sort the cards into groups. Label the boxes with different headings such as 'towns', 'beaches' and 'mountains'. By changing the headings you can vary the exercise. For example, you might get the children to sort the cards into summer and winter scenes.

Activity 27 Brochures

Materials needed
Holiday brochures, large map of the United Kingdom, large map of Europe.

Ask the children if they went away on holiday. Can they bring to school brochures and other details about where they went? What was the name of the nearest town? Was it in the United Kingdom or abroad? What was the country or region? Find the different places on a map and work out the approximate distance. What type of transport did the children use? How did their parents choose the destination?

Activity 28 Map exhibition

Materials needed
A variety of different maps of the United Kingdom.

Make an exhibition of different maps of the United Kingdom. You could use brochures, posters, atlases, reference books and other sources. Discuss what the maps show and get the children to describe how they vary. Can the children recognise their own country? What is it called? Extend the work using **Copymaster 11** (Which Country?).

Activity 29 Comparisons

Materials needed
Two contrasting pictures or photographs.

Select two contrasting pictures or photographs of different places. Working as a class, get the children to list the different features they can see. Pin the pictures and words on a display board with a space in between. Now write down all the features of your own area in the centre of the display. Finally, make a comparison between the lists. How many features of your own area correspond with features in the places in the pictures? Draw lines linking them together.

Activity 30 Picture viewer

Materials needed
Tracing paper, library books.

Make a display of books from the school library that have pictures of mountains, rivers, towns, villages and other geographical features. Talk with the children about what they can see. Encourage close observation by getting them to make a simple picture viewer by drawing a grid on tracing paper, or some other transparent material. The grid should divide the picture into four sections – near and distant, left and right. What can the children find in each section? Can they imagine what the things in the distance might look like from close to?

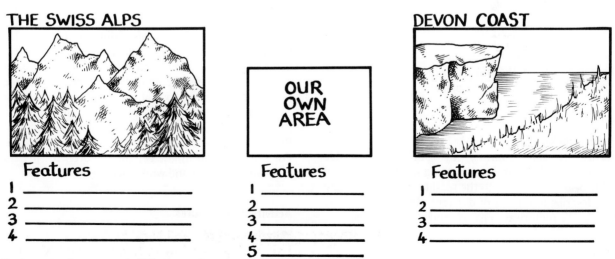

Compare pictures of different places.

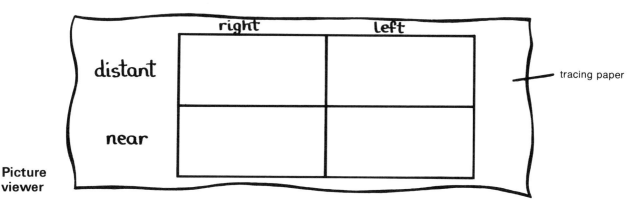

Picture viewer

tracing paper

Activity 31 Library quiz

Materials needed
Library books, quiz cards.

Select some library books which have a variety of pictures showing places around the world. Devise some quiz cards to go with the books. For example, you might ask the children which book has a picture of the River Nile in it, or what they can see on the cover of a given book. You could turn this activity into a game in which the children describe a picture as clearly as they can without naming it, while the others guess what it is. Both approaches will help to extend the children's geographical vocabulary and enhance their powers of visual discrimination.

Activity 32 Other countries

Materials needed
Pictures from magazines.

Make a display of pictures from magazines showing different places around the world. These could include cities, motorways, forests, deserts and villages. Discuss the pictures with the children. What do they show? Is it a place in our own country, or is it somewhere overseas? Use **Copymaster 12** (Features) to get the children to analyse the pictures in greater detail.

Activity 33 Stamps

Materials needed
Stamp collection from a number of different countries.

Put a selection of stamps from different countries out on display in the classroom. Can the children work out which country each stamp comes from? Ask the children to sort them into sets, using labels for the different countries. Do they have any stamps at home that they could contribute to the display?

Stamps: make a stamp collection

11

MAPWORK

All maps interpret the world selectively. Political maps, for example, show the boundaries between countries. A mariner's chart, by contrast, provides information about ocean currents and the depth of the sea bed. Today, almost any kind of information can be presented in map form. Maps are increasingly being used to provide information on environmental and social issues such as population growth, pollution and deforestation.

The problem facing all map-makers is how to represent the Earth, which is three-dimensional, on a two-dimensional piece of paper. The solution lies in the use of mathematical grids or projections. One of the most famous projections was devised by Mercator in the sixteenth century to guide the exploration of the earth. In recent times Arno Peters has popularised a projection which, unlike Mercator's, is accurate in terms of area. This has been favoured by many aid agencies as it challenges Eurocentric perceptions.

In teaching children how to use maps, it is best to begin with large-scale maps of the local area. The classroom, school building and grounds provide a safe and familiar environment in which they can practise basic skills. Globes and world maps can be introduced as occasion permits to enhance the children's knowledge of distant places.

It is important to remember that all maps are designed to convey information. Children should therefore be introduced to maps in context and use them to support work in other projects. Journeys, rivers and weather are some of the themes which provide a natural link. There are also good opportunities for using maps alongside stories and fairy tales. For example, you could ask the children to draw a map to show what happens in Aesop's Fable of the Hare and the Tortoise.

Most of the maps drawn by young children tend to be strongly pictorial. At their simplest, they will show a sequence of events or features in the correct order. Egocentric and personal details are included alongside more objective information. Gradually children learn how to represent the world in a more formalised manner. Research shows that infants do not usually draw maps spontaneously. However, when given encouragement by a teacher they readily appreciate their value and often start drawing maps enthusiastically.

Map projections

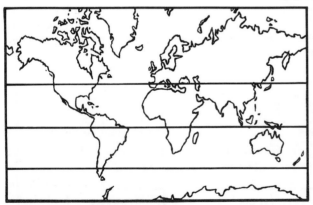

Mercator's projection shows direction accurately but enlarges the polar regions.

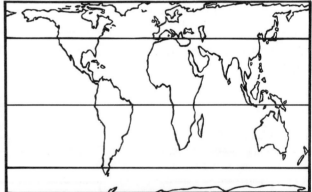

Peters' projection shows area accurately but distorts the shape of the continents.

Pupils should be taught to follow directions, including the terms up, down, on, under, behind, in front of, near, far, left, right, north, south, east, west.

Progression indicators
- know simple directional vocabulary
- follow directions to another part of the school
- use a magnetic compass or programmable toy

Interpretation
Pupils should be able to follow directions round the classroom, school building and school site. They should be introduced to large scale plans and use specific equipment such as a magnetic compass or a programmable toy.

Introduction

One of the first skills that very young children learn is how to cope with their immediate physical surroundings. They become aware of the location of objects within the first few months of their lives. As they grow older, children come to realise that the external world has a permanent existence.

Young children are highly egocentric and define the position of objects in relation to themselves. For example, a baby girl lying in her cot may have her teddy in front of her and her rattle above her. When she stands up and turns round this spatial relationship alters. As they grow older, infants still find spatial awareness a problem because they use a wider range of directional vocabulary and they move in more complex surroundings.

This unit requires children to follow directions, which means they must apply their knowledge. It also implies that they are able to follow instructions. This is one of the requirements of the English curriculum. There is a range of specific vocabulary which children will need to use if they are to cope with these demands.

Key vocabulary

above	east	on
backwards	far	right
behind	forwards	south
below	in front of	under
compass	left	up
direction	near	west
down	north	

Key questions

Who follows directions?
Have you ever given directions?
What things show directions?
What happens to people when they lose their sense of direction?

Resources

Picture books

The Journey Home by Joanne Plindall (Walker, 1988) is ideal for supporting work on directions. Each double-page spread shows a family driving home through a landscape. There are plenty of things to talk about and discuss with the children.

Rhymes

The Grand Old Duke of York

Oh, the Grand Old Duke of York,
He had ten thousand men;
He marched them up to the top of the hill,
And he marched them down again.
Now when they were up, they were up;
And when they were down, they were down;
But when they were only half-way up,
They were neither up nor down.

Mr East gave a Feast

Mr East gave a feast,
Mr North laid the cloth,
Mr West did his best,
Mr South burnt his mouth
With eating a cold potato

Songs

'The Bear went over the Mountain', from *Apusskidu* by Beatrice Harrop (Black, 1975) helps to re-inforce directional vocabulary.

Activity 34 Direction words

Working from the key vocabulary list, decide which directional words the children need to learn. Use these words in as many practical situations as possible. You could get the children to follow directions when they want to find things in class, when you are playing games in the hall, or to point things out on an environmental walk. Reinforce the work by playing a game of 'Simon Says'. Are there any direction words which make interesting clapping patterns in time to music?

Activity 35 Blindfold donkey game

Materials needed

Scarf or other material to make a blindfold and 'tail'.

Play the blindfold donkey game either with groups of children or with the whole class. You will need to select one child to be the donkey. The child is then blindfolded and given a tail. Other children call out directions for the donkey to follow. These should specify the number of paces as well as the direction. The challenge is for the child to follow the instructions correctly. You can play the game as a time-filler when you have a few minutes to spare at the end of a lesson. As the children get more experienced, you can make the instructions more complicated.

Activity 36 Model farm

Materials needed

Toy farm buildings and animals, instruction cards.

Make some instruction cards for the children to use when they play with toy buildings and animals. The instructions should use directional words, and help the children to construct a model of a farm. You might ask them to put the cat in front of the shed, or the horse in the field. When the children are familiar with the layout you can change the instructions. You could also ask them to bring some toys of their own to add to the scene.

Activity 37 Arrows

Materials needed

Light card, scissors.

Play some direction games using arrows. Cut these out from light card. Get the children to lay the arrows on the floor to show the way to the sink, home corner, library corner or other points of interest. Ask the children to describe the routes they have made up. Now remove the arrows and see if a child can reach the correct destination by following the instructions only.

Activity 38 Left and right

Materials needed
Ribbons of different colours, crayons, paper.

Give the children ribbons to tie on to their wrists. They should have two different colours, one for the left and the other for the right. Get them to make a drawing showing things to the left and right of where they sit. They can colour the things to match the colour of their ribbons and write the words left and right in large letters at the top of their drawings.

Activity 39 Left and right stick

Materials needed
Some light sticks, scissors, card, Sellotape.

Get the children to draw round their hands on a piece of card. They should then label the shapes 'left' and 'right', cut them out and fix them to the end of a light stick using Sellotape. Working in pairs, the children can now go on short journeys with their sticks. One of the children should call out directions, such as 'Turn right', while the other, who holds the stick, obeys them like a

Direction finder. Make a direction finder by fixing the arrow to the cardboard circle with a paper fastener.

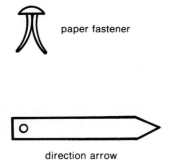

paper fastener

direction arrow

robot. After a while the children should swap places so they both get a turn at following instructions.

Activity 40 Left and right survey
Do a survey on left and right by looking at things in the classroom. How many pieces of furniture have catches or handles on the left? How many have them on the right? How many children are left-handed? When you go on a classroom journey, how many times do you turn left and right? **Copymaster 13** (Left and Right Survey) has been designed to help children record their answers. You might also make a class display of the findings in the form of a table and pictures.

6 children write with their left hand.

20 children write with their right hand.

HANDS

left	6
right	20

Activity 41 Direction finder

Materials needed
Light card, paper fasteners, scissors.

Get the children to make a simple direction finder. They will need to cut out a circle about 10 cm in diameter from light card. They should then write the words 'go forward', 'go back', 'turn left', 'turn right' at the correct points and fix an arrow to the centre with a paper fastener. By turning the arrow the children will be able to give themselves instructions and create routes round the classroom. The direction finder will encourage them to make 90° turns. It will also help to reinforce the idea of left and right.

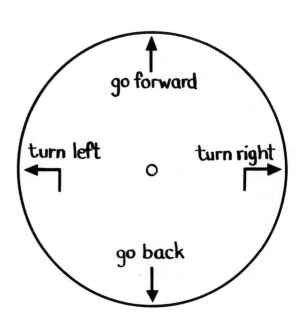

go forward

turn left   turn right

go back

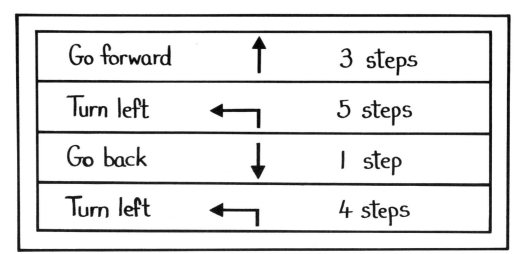

Go forward	↑	3 steps
Turn left	←	5 steps
Go back	↓	1 step
Turn left	←	4 steps

Instructions for a mystery trail

Activity 42 Mystery trail

Materials needed

Direction finders (see activity 41), light card, dice.

Make up some routes for the children to follow using their direction finders. You could write down the instructions on pieces of card. Where does each route lead to? Are there any obstacles that get in the way? You could extend the activity by letting the children fill in the number of steps that they are going to take in each direction by throwing a dice.

Activity 43 Programmable toy

Materials needed

Programmable toy or robot (e.g. Big Trak, Turtle, Roamer), computer, computer program.

Set up a programmable toy or robot which the children can play with in groups. When they have got used to the equipment you can ask them to work out a program for it to follow. This might involve going forwards, backwards, left and right. Enter the program into the computer and see if it works in practice. What other programs can the children devise for the toy to follow?

A programmable toy and computer

Activity 44 Signs in school

Materials needed

Card, artwork materials.

Look round your school to see if you can discover any arrows or direction signs. What do they tell you? Are they easy to follow? Discuss any signs which it might be useful to have either in your school or class. Make them out of card and fix them to suitable places. You might have signs pointing to the book corner, sink, places to put rubbish, and so on.

Activity 45 School journeys

Materials needed

Large plan of the school, felt pens.

Make a large plan of the school for a wall display. Use this to record any journeys that the children make around the school during the day. For example, you might ask a child to deliver a message to another class or take the register to the secretary. With your help the children should draw their route on the wall map. Mark each route in a different colour and identify what it represents in a key. Which parts of the school are busiest? Are there any places which the children never seem to visit? Use **Copymaster 14** (Routes) to develop the idea that colour helps to pick out or distinguish different routes.

Activity 46 Signs in the street

Take the children on a walk in the streets near your school to see how traffic signs are used. How many can they find? What do they tell us? Discuss each one in turn. You could get the children to record their findings in drawings, or give them **Copymaster 15** (Street Signs) to complete. Find out more about traffic signs when you return to school. *The Highway Code* is one of the best reference sources. You could either use this directly or make up a reference sheet illustrating a few important signs.

Activity 47 Street trail

Materials needed

Duplicated sketch maps of the trail route (camera and film – optional).

Devise a simple walk in the area immediately surrounding the school. Write down the main buildings and other places that the children will pass on the route. Mark them on a simple sketch map of the trail and duplicate copies so that every child has one of their own. As the children go round the route, get them to keep track of their position. Ask them whether to turn left or right at junctions. See if they can identify the

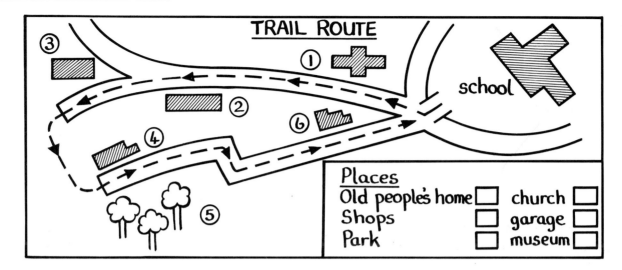

places you have marked using a number system. You might also take photographs for use in a large picture plan when you return to school.

Activity 48 Compass directions

Materials needed
Compass, sugar paper.

Using a compass, find out which way is north, south, east and west from your classroom. Write large direction labels on some sheets of sugar paper and pin them to the correct walls. Talk about the different compass directions with the children. What can they see to the north of them? What can they see to the south? Repeat this exercise in the hall or playground. You could ask the children to record their findings either in words or pictures, using **Copymaster 16** (Compass Directions). Extend the work in direction and movement games. Can the children touch the north wall, point to the east wall, and so on?

Activity 49 Make a compass

Materials needed
Card, scissors, crayons, paper fasteners, compass.

Get the children to make their own compass. They could either colour and cut out the compass in **Copymaster 17** (Compass Model), or you could provide them with a compass cut-out of your own. When they have cut out the compass shape they should add a 'needle' by fixing an arrow to the middle of the compass with a paper fastener. The children can align their models with a real compass at different points around the school. This will reinforce the idea of the different directions and help them to understand how a real compass is used.

Activity 50 North and South Pole

Materials needed
Globe or world map.

Talk to the children about where you would get to if you kept on travelling north. Do they have any ideas? Look at a globe or world map to find the arctic and lands of the north. Explain that the Earth is a sphere which spins in space. Which two places stay stationary? What are they called? What are the differences between the North and South Poles?

Make a compass by fixing the compass 'needle' to the template with a paper fastener.

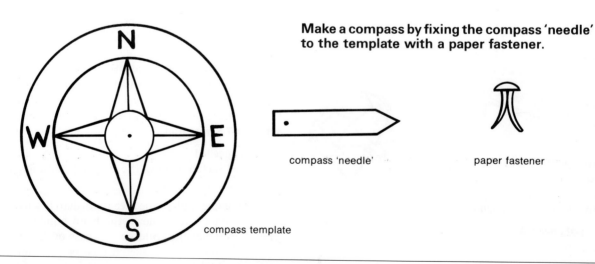

compass 'needle'

paper fastener

compass template

Blueprints links
See sheet 35, Direction, in the *Infant Geography Resource Bank*.

MAKE MAPS AND PLANS ▶

Pupils should be taught to make maps and plans of real and imaginary places, using pictures and symbols, *eg a pictorial map of a place featured in a story, a plan of their route from home to school.*

Progression indicators
- draw round objects to make a plan
- draw pictorial maps of places in a story
- draw some of the features of the journey to school in sequence

Interpretation
The children draw plan views of familiar objects, make maps or pictures of their classroom and other familiar environments and represent imaginary places such as a treasure island.

Introduction
Mapwork is the most distinctive geographical skill. The ability to make a permanent visual record of the environment is one of the most significant human achievements. It has enabled people to record journeys and voyages, identify their location and communicate information about distant places. Maps have played a key role in the development of knowledge, and must rank alongside the invention of the wheel in allowing people to break out of their immediate surroundings, conquer distance and dominate the planet.

There are two main types of map. Conventional maps portray the world according to a number of agreed rules which include the use of symbols, scale and orientation. Conceptual maps, on the other hand, are much more personal. These are the maps we carry in our heads and which enable us to find our way from one place to another.

This unit focuses on conceptual mapping. It encourages children to draw their own plans or pictures of different places, both familiar and unfamiliar. These should indicate spatial relationships, but need not follow set rules. The children will be fascinated by the problem of representing three-dimensional reality on a two-dimensional piece of paper.

Key vocabulary
above	landmark	scale
code	map	shape
direction	north	sign
grid	plan	symbol
key	route	way

Key questions
What things are shown on maps and plans?
What is the difference between a picture and a plan?
What different types of maps are there?
Who uses maps and plans?

Resources

Fairy tales
Most fairy tales require children to develop a mental image of the place where they are set. This provides an excellent opportunity to present the story through picture maps. Here are some suggestions:

Snow White Make a class collage to show the places in the story.
Hansel and Gretel What route did the children take through the forest?
Jack and the Bean Stalk Get the children to draw a plan of the giant's room.
Cinderella Create a sequence of drawings to show the events in the story.
Little Red Riding Hood Make a picture map of Red Riding Hood's journey.
The Emperor's New Clothes Design a route for a procession in your own neighbourhood.

Picture books
Some picture books describe routes and landmarks. *Rosie's Walk* by Pat Hutchins (Bodley, 1968) is one of the most well-known. *Spot's First Walk* by Eric Hill (Heinemann, 1981) is another suitable book. Adventure stories can provide more open-ended opportunities. *The Baron on the Island of Cheese* by Adrian Mitchell (Walker, 1986) is one of a series of tales which involve journeys around the world. These appeal to older children.

Activity 51 Overhead projector

Materials needed
Toy vehicles, models and other small objects, overhead projector, paper.

Collect together a number of different objects that have interesting plans. Small toys and everyday objects are ideal. Place them, one at a time, on an overhead projector and shine the image on to the wall. Can the children guess the object from its plan? Why are plans always drawn from directly overhead? Pin some paper on the wall and get the children to draw round the shapes and cut them out for a class display. Are the children still able to recognise the different plans? Get them to write labels before they forget what the plans are of.

Activity 52 Plan views

Materials needed
A selection of everyday items, camera and film.

Take photographs of some everyday objects such as a saucepan, cup, table lamp and iron. You will need to

overhead projector

roll of Sellotape

paper

shadow plan view

Place different classroom objects on an OHP and project their plan shapes on to a wall.

take two photographs of each thing: one to show the side view (elevation), and the other to show the overhead view (plan). If possible, mount the photographs on card and cover them for protection. Talk with the children about what they can see in each photograph. Does it show the view from above, or a side view? Can they sort the photographs into sets and match them with the objects? Ask them to draw the plan view for themselves. Use **Copymaster 18** (Plan Views) to develop the work.

Activity 53 Tray game

Materials needed
A number of objects and labels, tray, light card, scissors.

Place a number of objects on a tray. Ask the children to make a plan of each one by drawing round the outline on to a piece of card. Get them to cut out the shapes. See if they can make plans which match the objects on the tray. When you have checked that they are correct, the children should add labels saying what each shape represents. You can repeat the game on a number of different occasions, adding more objects each time so that it becomes more complicated.

Activity 54 Class plan

Materials needed
Large class plan, small pieces of card.

Make a large class plan for a wall display. Talk about it with the children. Can they identify the windows, door, teacher's table, and so on? Ask them to write their name on a piece of card and pin it to the correct place

on the plan to show where they sit. Add other labels to indicate the activity areas, for example the art corner and book corner. When the children are familiar with the plan you could use it for some class games. Move the names around before the children come into school and get them to work out where they must go and sit. Alternatively, you could ask all the children in the class to sit in different places. The children then have to make the plan match up with their new positions.

Activity 55 Signpost map

Materials needed
Classroom plans.

Either ask the children to draw a simple plan of the classroom, or duplicate one for them to use. Get them to put a cross to mark where they are sitting. They should then draw arrows to key points in the classroom such as the windows, door, teacher's desk and sink, and label them. Not only will this help the children to orientate themselves, it also gives them further experience in using a class plan.

Activity 56 Journey plan

Materials needed
Paper, crayons, felt tips, plasticine.

Ask the children to make a plan or picture of their journey to school. This should show the things that they pass, any important road crossings, and sharp turns or changes in direction. It is important to talk with the children about what they are going to show before they begin the work, but equally they need to be given a free hand and not constrained in how they choose to represent the route. Encourage them to add details to

Tray game. See if the children can match the objects on a tray with their plan shape.

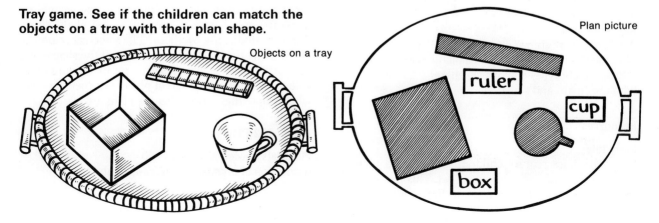

Objects on a tray

Plan picture

ruler

cup

box

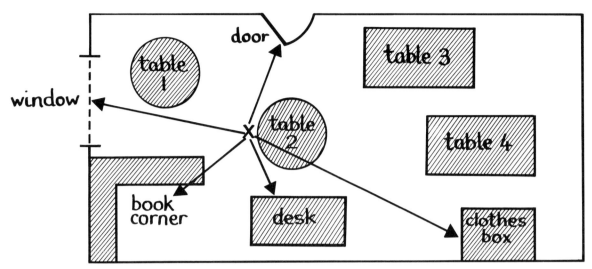

Signpost map. Ask the children to draw arrows from the place where they sit to different parts of the room.

their plans as they remember things that they have left out. You might extend the exercise by asking the children to make a simple plasticine model based on their plans. You could follow up this work with **Copymaster 19** (Route Maze).

Activity 57 Scenes

Materials needed
Play mats, toy vehicles, farm animals, Lego.

Make or buy a series of play mats showing road patterns, farm layouts, and so on. Get the children to devise scenes using the mats as a base, and the toys from the play cupboard. When they are satisfied with a scene, ask the children to record the layout as a plan or picture on a piece of paper. Pack the materials away and see if the children can replace the pieces exactly as they were before, working from their drawings. As a variation, you could provide the children with plans that they have to follow as accurately as they can. **Copymaster 20** (Farm Scene) provides a linked extension exercise.

Activity 58 Adventure playground

Materials needed
Paper, crayons, scissors, glue.

Discuss with the children what equipment they would like to find in an adventure playground. They might suggest trampolines, assault courses, climbing frames, creatures to play on, a sandpit, ropes or swings. Ask them to do drawings of these different things, cut them out and arrange them on a plan. Discuss how they might be best positioned. How could the playground be made safe? Will there be somewhere for toddlers to play,

as well as an area for older children? **Copymaster 21** (Adventure Playground) provides some drawings which children can colour and add to their plans if they run out of ideas.

Activity 59 Adventure story

Get the children to make up an adventure story about a journey or voyage at sea. What happens? What different places do they visit? Are there disasters or dangers they have to face? Ask the children to show their story as a map or picture. They might make a sequence of linked drawings, or a unified scene in which all the different things take place. They should add notes round the edge explaining the details.

Activity 60 Treasure islands

Materials needed
Drawing paper, crayons, paints, chicken wire, newspaper, cold-water paste, thick card.

Create a map of an imaginary treasure island. Get the children to make up names for some of the different places – Misty Mountains, Deadman's Swamp, and so on. Ask them to add small drawings showing what they look like. Extend the work by making a class model from papier mâché. You will need a sheet of thick card for the base, and some chicken wire or screwed-up newspaper for the relief features. All the children can join in, glueing strips of newspaper to the model and building up different areas. The work will take several weeks to complete as the papier mâché should be allowed to dry out at intervals. The final stage is to paint the land and sea and label key features.

Blueprints links
Copymasters 36–40 in the *Infant Geography Resource Bank* provide picture maps to go with well-known stories and rhymes including *Sleeping Beauty* which is based on the Chateau d'Ussé near Chinon in France.

USE GLOBES, MAPS AND PLANS

Pupils should be taught to use globes, maps and plans at a variety of scales; the work should include identifying major geographical features, *eg seas, rivers, cities,* locating and naming on a map the constituent countries of the United Kingdom, marking on a map approximately where they live, and following a route.

Progression indicators
- know that there are different types of map
- recognise the shape of the British Isles
- locate where they live on a map

Interpretation
The children should use large-scale maps of their area, smaller scale maps, atlases and globes. They should know that the United Kingdom is made up of England, Wales, Scotland and Northern Ireland and be able to locate their own area.

Introduction
The United Kingdom is a political unit. It is made up of England, Wales, Scotland and Northern Ireland. The United Kingdom has developed over a long period of time. The last major step in the process was the Irish Treaty of 1921, when Northern Ireland was formed.

This unit raises questions about the features that distinguish a nation. With infants it is best to focus on visible clues such as the national flag and capital city. Maps and atlases will be a valuable source of information.

You will need to distinguish between the United Kingdom and the British Isles. As both terms are in common use some children may question the difference. The British Isles are a physical, not a political, unit and this is the term used for the group of islands which lie off the north-west coast of the European mainland. They are Great Britain (England, Scotland and Wales), Ireland, the Orkney and Shetland Islands, the Isle of Man, the Scilly Isles, the Isle of Wight and the Channel Islands.

Vocabulary

atlas	map	England
country	plan	Northern Ireland
flag	route	Scotland
globe	world	United Kingdom
		Wales

Key questions
What are the different countries of the United Kingdom?
Why are different types of map needed?
What does a globe show?

Resources

Atlases
There is a variety of atlases available for infants. Two popular ones are the *Keystart First Atlas* (Collins-Longman, 1990) and the *Oxford Infant Atlas* (Oxford, 1991) which is now also produced in an interactive version for use with an Acorn computer.

Globes
Inflatable globes are cheaper than traditional globes and the plastic surface makes them extremely versatile. The *Infant Globes* (Collins-Longman, 1995) comes with re-useable labels and pictures which can be fixed to the surface as required. You might also consider obtaining transparent globes which just show the outline of the continents and are even more versatile.

Activity 61 Footprints

Materials needed
Paper, light card, scissors, duplicated plans of the classroom.

Get the children to draw the outline of their feet on to a piece of card. They should then cut out the shapes in paper to create footprints, and place these around the class to show different routes. When each child has devised a route, ask them to mark it on a plan of the classroom. See if other children can follow it. What things do they pass on their journey? Do they have to take any sharp turns? If so, why? **Copymaster 22** (Tracks) extends the idea by looking at animal tracks.

Activity 62 Follow the route

Materials needed
Route cards, duplicated plans of the school, class book.

Make a series of route cards for the children to follow. These might ask them to go to the hall, staffroom, library, secretary's office and other suitable locations. Get the children to note the things they pass on the way, and the number of paces that they take to reach their destination. When they return to the class, ask the children to mark their route on a duplicated plan of the school. Can they think of any other way of getting to the same place? Was there a short cut that they might have taken? What obstacles got in the way? Mount the plans in a class book to make a route atlas.

Footprints. Get the children to devise a route for others to follow.

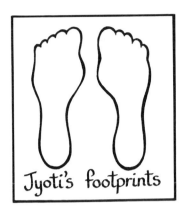

Jyoti's footprints

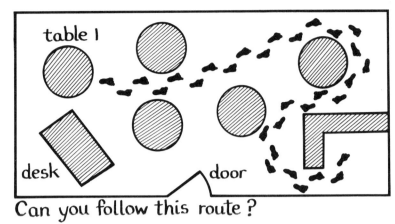

Can you follow this route?

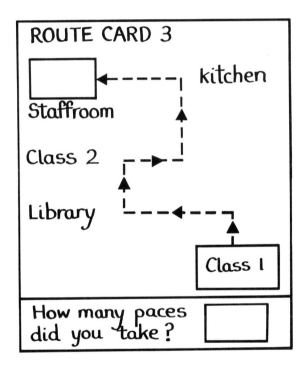

ROUTE CARD 3

kitchen

Staffroom

Class 2

Library

Class 1

How many paces did you take?

Activity 63 Tourist maps

Materials needed
Picture and tourist maps.

Look at some picture or tourist maps of your own area. What are the features which are shown? Ask the children to make their own drawings for a class wall map. Get them to add labels or descriptions. Can the children think of any other features they would like to add? Look at picture maps of other places in other parts of the country. What do these tell you about the places? Would you like to go there?

Activity 64 Journeys

Materials needed
Map of the local area, counters.

Help the children to find where they live on a map of the area. You could then ask them to plan a journey to a place of interest. Get them to show the route by placing counters on the map. Could they reach their destination in more than one way? Do they think that the shortest route is bound to be the quickest? Ask them to record their route using **Copymaster 23** (Journeys). Plan a number of other journeys to different locations in a similar way.

Activity 65 On the road

Materials needed
Paper, crayons or felt tips.

Ask the children to make a map showing a road linking two places. Get them to add as many details as they like. For example, they could show mountains, rivers, gorges, estuaries, swamps and other natural hazards. You should then ask them to list or describe what you would see on a journey between the two places. Alternatively, you could use **Copymaster 24** (On the Road). This takes a similar theme but provides a structure for the children to follow.

Activity 66 Name plates

Materials needed
Magazines and colour supplements, card, scissors, glue, sugar paper.

Give the children a set of magazines and colour supplements. Get them to cut out letters to make the name of their country. They could look for interesting and unusual scripts. Ask the children to mount their 'name plates' on sugar paper and put them up on the wall as a display.

Activity 67 Acrostic

Materials needed

Squares of card and sugar paper.

Write the letters which spell the name of your country on separate squares of card. Ask the children to arrange them in the correct order, and then attach them to a sheet of sugar paper in a vertical line. Now ask the children to think of an item that comes from your country which begins with each different letter. Write these next to the appropriate letter, together with a simple drawing or picture. If the children want to complete an acrostic of their own you could ring the changes by making up an acrostic using place names from your own area.

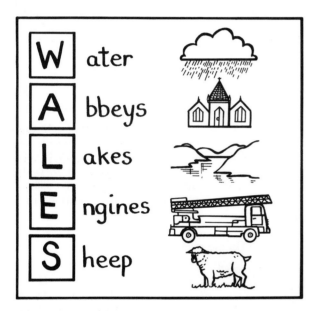

Activity 68 The British Isles

Materials needed

Map of the British Isles.

Look at a map of the British Isles with the children. Explain that the British Isles consist of lots of different islands. Encourage the children to identify key features on the map such as the rivers, lakes and mountains. Help them to locate their own position on the map.

Activity 69 Different countries

Materials needed

Flash cards, map of the United Kingdom, drawing pins.

Make up some flash cards with the names of the different countries of the United Kingdom written in capitals and small letters. Get the children to place them at the correct point on a map of the United Kingdom. How can they tell where one country ends and another begins? Which of the four parts of the United Kingdom is the largest? Which part is the smallest? Reinforce this activity using **Copymaster 25** (The United Kingdom).

Activity 70 Countries snap

Materials needed

Light card, felt tips.

Make some playing cards based on the names and outline shapes of the countries of the United Kingdom. You will need eight cards in each set – four for the names and four for the shape. Put several sets together to make a pack of cards and get the children to use them for games of snap. You could help to prepare the children for the game using **Copymaster 26** (Different Shapes).

Activity 71 Different flags

Materials needed

Map of the United Kingdom, gardening sticks, glue/Sellotape, scissors, plasticine.

Get the children to make flags for the different countries of the United Kingdom. **Copymasters 27** and **28** (Flags 1 and 2) provide outlines for the children to colour. They should cut these out and fix them to short poles made from gardening sticks. Lay out a map of the United Kingdom on the floor or some other horizontal surface and ask the children to plant the flags on the countries where they belong. A small lump of Plasticine makes a solid base and will stop the flags from falling over.

Activity 72 The Union Jack

Materials needed

A collection of items decorated with the Union Jack.

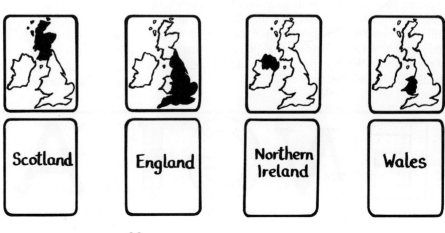

Cards for 'Countries snap'

22

Different flags

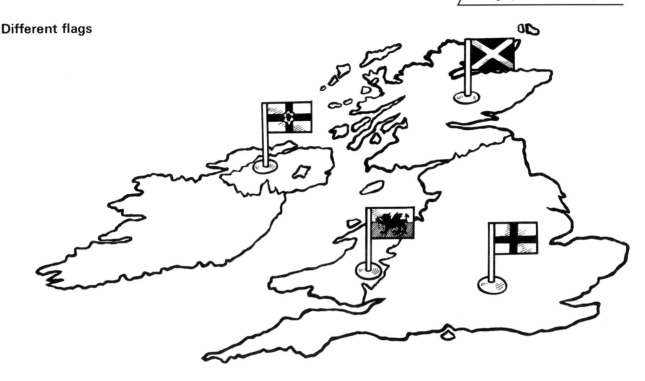

Explain to the class that the Union Jack is a combination of the flags of the different countries of the United Kingdom. Set up a display table with items that are decorated with the Union Jack. Examples might include tea towels, mugs, tins, pencils and other souvenirs. Encourage the children to contribute to the display. Discuss where you might see the Union Jack flying in your local area. When is it used?

Activity 73 Connections

Materials needed
Map of the United Kingdom.

Ask the children if they have any friends or relatives who live in a different part of the United Kingdom. Can they find where they live on a map? What country do they live in? Ask them to describe what it is like there. Is it crowded or empty, flat or hilly? Are there any important differences which the children can remember noticing?

Activity 74 Impressions

Materials needed
Large labels for the four parts of the United Kingdom, drawing pins.

Divide a display board into four sections, one for each part of the United Kingdom. Pin a label at the top of each section and ask the children to collect items for a class display. For example, the section on Scotland might include photographs of mountains and castles from magazines and calendars, tartan wrapping paper and a drawing of a Scotsman playing the bagpipes.

Activity 75 Countries game

Materials needed
Large labels, Sellotape, music.

Make large labels for each of the parts of the United Kingdom and put them up in the corners of the school hall before beginning a movement lesson. When the class is ready, play the children some music and ask them to dance. Every so often you should stop the music and call out the name of a country. The children then have to run to the correct corner. You can make the game more atmospheric by putting up flags as well.

Activity 76 Voices

Materials needed
Tape recorder, cassette.

Make up a tape recording of people speaking in the accent of their country. You might know people from different parts of the United Kingdom whom you could record speaking live. Alternatively, you might be able to find suitable cassettes in the local library. Play the cassette to the children and see if they can identify the accents. Extend the activity by reading the children stories and folk tales from different areas. Try to choose examples which capture the atmosphere of the place concerned.

Activity 77 Jigsaw puzzle

Materials needed
Jigsaw puzzle of the United Kingdom.

Ask the children to complete a jigsaw puzzle of the United Kingdom. You will find that you can purchase these from commercial suppliers if they are not available in your school. Can the children identify the country which they live in? Where is your own village or town? What is the nearest feature shown on the jigsaw? Extend the activity using **Copymaster 29** (UK Jigsaw).

Activity 78 Borders

Materials needed
Map of the United Kingdom.

Talk about the boundaries of your school. How do you

know where the school grounds finish and other land begins? Organise a walk around the edges of the site. What different types of border can you see? Get the children to record their observations on **Copymaster 30** (Borders), either working on their own or with the help of an adult. Look at a map of your country when you return to the classroom. In what places does the sea make a border? Where does the border cross the land?

Activity 79 Imaginary map
Ask the children to draw a map of an island divided into two different countries. The border might run along a river, cross a narrow neck of land or follow a mountain range. Talk with the children about the differences between the two countries. Can they think up names for them? Which one would they prefer to live in?

Activity 80 Capital cities

Materials needed
Map of Europe or the world.

Talk about capital cities with the children. What makes them special? What is the capital city of your own country? Look at a map of Europe or the world. Get the children to identify some different capital cities. How many have they heard of before? Have any of the children visited a capital city?

Activity 81 Name display

Materials needed
A variety of objects displaying the name of your country.

Set up a display table with a variety of objects, all of which feature the name of your country. These may be small items with the words 'Made in . . .' on the bottom, or tourists' souvenirs, such as brochures and tea towels. Can the children find the country name on each thing? Why has it been put there?

Activity 82 World map

Materials needed
Atlas or world map.

Look at a map of the world with the children using an atlas, poster or satellite image. What are the different continents and oceans called? Where are the Poles and the equator? Where is the British Isles? Use the map to discuss places the children have heard about. Think about rivers and cities, the different landscapes and the animals and creatures which live there.

Activity 83 Globe

Materials needed
Traditional or inflatable globe, coloured adhesive dots.

Show the children a globe and talk about the information which it shows. What are the main landscape features? How many different countries are shown? Use a transparent inflatable globe to collect information about the world. For example, the children could add coloured adhesive dots to show the places they have visited, to trace a journey around the world or to show events which they know about such as the Olympic Games and other sports contests.

Blueprints links
There is a set of base maps for the different parts of the UK and the world (Copymasters 26–34) in the *Infant Geography Resource Bank*.

PLACES

■ **4.** Two localities should be studied: the locality of the school and a locality, either in the United Kingdom or overseas, in which the physical and/or human features contrast with those in the locality of the school. The locality of the school is its immediate vicinity; it includes the school buildings and grounds and the surrounding area within easy access. The contrasting locality should be an area of similar size.

■ **5.** In these studies, pupils should be taught:

    a about the main physical and human features, *eg rivers, hills, factories, shops,* that give the localities their character;

    b how localities may be similar and how they may differ, *eg both areas may have farmland, but animals may be kept on the farms in one area, while in the other crops may be grown;*

    c about the effects of weather on people and their surroundings, *eg the effect of seasonal variations in temperature on the clothes people wear;*

    d how land buildings, *eg farms, parks, factories, houses,* are used.

The study of places is central to geography. The curriculum aims to help children understand what makes places distinctive and different from each other. During the course of their school careers children should also develop a broader and deeper knowledge of the wider world.

Geography is such a vast subject that it would be impossible to study all parts of the world in equal depth. The geography Order adopts a selective approach.

During Key Stage 1 children are required to study (a) the locality of the school and (b) a contrasting locality either somewhere else in the UK or overseas. The locality is specifically defined as the vicinity of the school or an area of equivalent size. However, although the work should be focused on a small area, children also need to learn how localities fit into a broader geographical context. This means that you can broaden the studies to take in other considerations.

THE SCHOOL LOCALITY

The local environment is a rich teaching resource. Even the most ordinary looking side street can be full of geographical interest. Not only will it provide information about local rocks and soils and the shape of the landscape, it will also show how people have used their surroundings either for houses and shops or for other facilities such as parks and churches.

Geography is essentially a practical subject and children gain a great deal from observing and recording information about their locality at first hand. Much of the work at Key Stage 1 will be concerned with developing vocabulary and learning specific terminology. Sorting and classification activities will also be important, particularly with older infants.

When they study the local area the children need to study both physical and human features. One way of defining physical features is to think of them as those aspects of the environment which are independent of people and would happen whether or not a place is inhabited. Conversely, human features are to do with the way people have responded to their surroundings. (See figure 1).

One way of structuring the work is to focus on geographical enquiries. Questions such as 'What is this place like?' 'How is it changing?' and 'What is it like to

Physical Features		Human Features	
hills	ponds	houses	roads
valleys	streams	shops	railways
woods	lakes	churches	paths
slopes	rivers	parks	bridges
rocks	marshes	museums	stations
wind	estuaries	factories	garages
rain	beaches	workshops	recycling points
temperature	cliffs	hospitals	nature reserves
	seashores	schools	

Figure 1 Physical and human features in the local area.

live in?' can help to provide a focus. They also suggest a line of investigation which children will need to pursue in order to find the answer.

When children have studied their own environment they will then be able to make meaningful comparisons with other parts of the world. Over a period of time their perception and understanding will mature and they will become increasingly geographically literate. The foundations need to be laid in the first years of schooling.

Two localities should be studied: the locality of the school and a locality either in the United Kingdom or overseas. The locality of the school is its immediate vicinity; it includes the school buildings and grounds and the surrounding area within easy access.

Progression indicators
- talk about features of the school buildings and grounds
- name a variety of places in the local area
- describe the jobs and activities in different local buildings

Interpretation
The children should find out about the weather, water, streams and woods near their school. They should also learn about houses, shops, places of work and leisure facilities.

Introduction

By the time they come to school, children will already be familiar with different aspects of the local area. They will have a detailed knowledge of their own home, they will have made regular visits to the shops and they will have used various play facilities.

This unit builds on and extends the children's knowledge. It focuses on the school building and immediate vicinity. One advantage of this approach is that there are good opportunities for direct experience and fieldwork. Another is that geographical ideas are illustrated in a scale and context which relates to the child's understanding.

You will need a number of resources in order to develop the work to its full potential. Perhaps the most essential single item is a large-scale map of the school environment. The Ordnance Survey 1:1,250 scale superplans are ideal. Photographs of local features and an aerial photograph of the local area are also extremely useful. However, the things which children can see and experience for themselves are the most important resource of all and they have the advantage of being completely free.

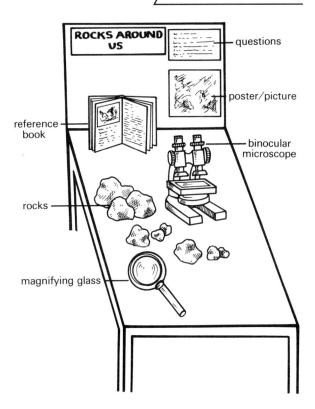

Key vocabulary

address	park
area	playground
bridge	post box
bus stop	school
church	shop
country	stream
envelope	street
factory	town
hill	wood
guide	village

Key questions

What are the main buildings and landmarks in the local area?
What are the names of local streets and places?
How are different buildings used?
Can they be put into categories?

Resources

Rhymes

Mother Goose Comes to Cable Street by Rosemary Stones and Andrew Mann (Kestrel, 1977) is a beautifully illustrated collection of modern nursery rhymes in an urban setting.

Picture books

Wilberforce Goes to Playgroup by Margaret Gordon (Penguin, 1987) is one of a series of stories about Wilberforce the bear, all of which are set in an everyday environment. The pictures are full of details for the children to observe and discuss.

Activity 84 Rock collection

Materials needed

Rock collection, magnifying glass, binocular microscope, reference books.

Set up a collection of local rocks and stones. If possible include some fossils and a variety of different colours and textures. Get the children to contribute by bringing in their own examples. Have a magnifying glass and, if possible, a binocular microscope to hand so that the children can examine the collection properly. As well as sorting the rocks into groups, the children might identify them in simple reference books and discuss where they come from.

Activity 85 Investigating the school grounds

Materials needed

Plastic bottles, margarine tubs with lids, plastic bags.

Look for different examples of rocks, soil and water in the school grounds. You could take some containers with you for collecting what you discover. Use plastic bags for pebbles and stones, margarine tubs for soil and plastic bottles for water from puddles. Bring what you have collected back to the class and set up a display. Add labels saying where each item came from.

Activity 86 Different soils

Materials needed

Samples of different types of soil, jars or transparent bottles.

Collect samples of soil from different places around the school or neighbourhood. Try to include gritty

Different soils. Study soil samples from different places around the school.

soil, clay, dust, and so on. Return any living creatures that you find so that they are not disturbed. Use the soil samples for some simple experiments. Can the soil be rolled into a ball like Plasticine? What are the differences in colour between the samples? What happens when the soil is mixed with water? Get the children to make a display of jars or bottles so they can see how the soil samples settle after they have been mixed and shaken with water.

Activity 87 Streets

Materials needed
Large-scale map of the local area, pins, photographs of street name plates.

Pin a large-scale map of the local area on to the classroom wall. Get the children to find the street where they live and mark it with a pin. Ask them to write the different names in the style of a road name plate, and add these to the display. It is helpful if you have some photographs for the children to copy.

Activity 88 Street names
Talk with the children about local street names. Are they named after geographical features (such as hills),

famous people, places, or different animals? If they had to make up a name for a new street near the school, what would they choose? Find out more about where the children live using **Copymaster 31** (Street Names). Ask individual children to call out the name of their street, while the rest colour in a box in the correct column.

Activity 89 Name rubbings

Materials needed
Set of template letters, wax crayons of different colours, plasticine.

Cut out a set of template letters from a sheet of card. Ask the children to use these to make up a name plate for their street. Get them to fix the letters down loosely with plasticine so that they can take a rubbing. You can then mount the rubbings on the wall as a class display. If you give the children crayons of different colours they can experiment with different effects. You can also use a variety of different papers to create extra interest and contrast.

Activity 90 Where we live

Materials needed
Ordnance Survey map of the locality, crayons, paper, string or wool.

When the children go home in the afternoon, ask them to take a careful look at their homes so that they can draw them the next day. Get them to look especially at the number on the door, the number of windows and the shape of the roof. Ask the children to make their drawings using crayons and paper. Arrange the pictures on the wall around a map of the locality. Join them to the correct place on the map using string or wool. Write underneath, *We live in a village/town/city*. Complete **Copymaster 32** (Where I live) as a way of extending the work.

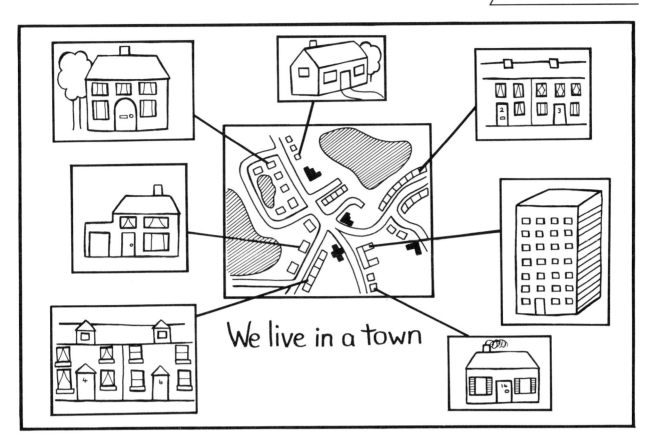

Activity 91 Picture map

Materials needed
Large-scale map of the local area.

Draw a large-scale map of the local area as a wall display. Begin with just an outline of the local streets. Get the children to identify the position of the school and see how many different places they can name. Ask them to make drawings of familiar features to add to the map. They might show their own homes, local churches, traffic lights, shops, street signs, and so on. Discuss the map with the whole class. What impression does it give of your neighbourhood? **Copymaster 33** (Building survey) will help the children find out if any things have been missed out.

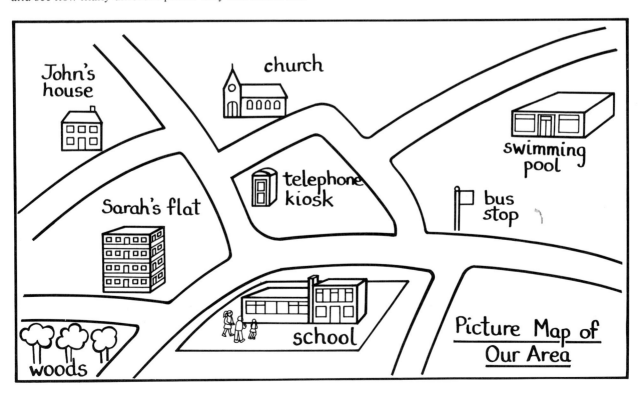

Activity 92 Local goods and services

Materials needed

Map of the local area, card for labels.

Talk with the children about the different goods and services which are produced in your area. A country area will have farms, on the coast there could be fishing, along rivers gravel works are quite common, towns have industrial buildings and factories. Do the children know the location of the nearest power station, reservoir, main post office, milk depot, and so on? Make some labels and pin them on to a map at the correct point.

Activity 93 Places snap

Materials needed

Photographs of familiar features in the locality, labels and light card.

Take a set of photographs of familiar features in the immediate locality and mount them on light card. Now make a set of card labels of the same size, naming each feature. Use the photographs and labels to play places snap. You will need to show the children all the photographs and labels before they begin the game. They will consolidate their knowledge of local places as they play it.

Activity 94 Landmarks

Materials needed

Frieze paper, scissors, crayons, glue.

Consider the landmarks which different people notice. Car drivers see road signs, elderly people know where to find seats and benches, tourists look out for museums and other attractions. Develop this idea using **Copymaster 34** (Landmarks). The children should colour the pictures, cut them out and arrange them as a frieze. They might also add some drawings of their own.

Activity 95 Places alphabet

Materials needed

Pieces of light card.

Working as a class, make a list of all the places you can think of in the local area. Get the children to write a label for each one on a piece of card. Mount these in alphabetical order as a class display. Extend the work by asking the children to complete **Copymaster 35** (Places Alphabet). There are spaces for eight letters on the street. You could either choose these beforehand or let the children make their own selection.

Activity 96 Guide book

Materials needed

Photographs of local features, glue, class book.

Make a guide book for your local area. You will need to collect a range of different photographs or pictures of local features for the children to use. Get them to name each one and mount it in a class book, together with a caption. If there is any spare space you could include some drawings which the children have made. These are best made on site as part of an organised visit or outing.

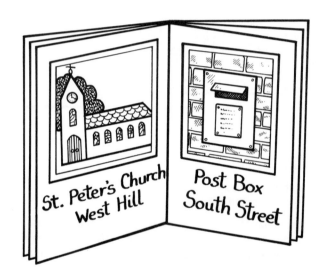

Activity 97 Places quiz

Materials needed

Quiz cards, empty shoe box.

Make a series of quiz cards which involve local landmarks and other features. For example, you might ask the children to name the local park, or the nearest street with a post box. You could put the questions in a special quiz box for the children to use in conjunction with the class guide book (see Activity 96).

VISITING LOCAL STREETS

Wherever your school is situated there will be plenty of opportunities to use local streets to develop basic geographical skills and knowledge. A short walk, planned round a circular route if possible, gives children the chance to observe their surroundings, ask questions and develop appropriate vocabulary.

You can focus on a range of themes including houses, shops, jobs, plants, creatures and the environment. Depending on the circumstances you could ask the children to make drawings, take photographs or collect items for a display table. You can also enhance the study by looking at a large-scale Ordnance Survey map of the area.

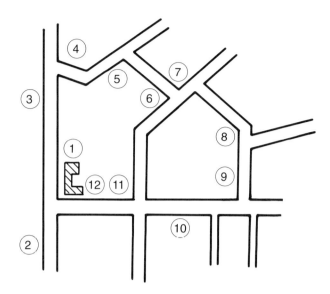

1. The School
How do people know the name of the school?
Where is the entrance?
Who works in the school apart from teachers?

2. Factory
What is the factory called?
What does it make?

3. Advertisements
What do the posters say?
Who passes the advertisements?

4. Shop
What does the shop sell?
When is it open?

5. Houses
Are the houses detached, semi-detached, terraced, flats or bungalows?

6. Post Box
What is the post box used for?
Who makes sure it works?
How often is the box emptied?

7. Pedestrian Crossing
Why is the crossing needed?
When is the road busiest?

8. Play Area
What can you do in the play area?
Who uses it?
Is it a place that you like?

9. Street Signs
How do we know the name of a road?
What do other street signs tell us?

10. Building Site
What is being built?
What machines can you see?
What jobs are people doing?

11. School Sign
Why is the sign placed here?
Who decided to put signs up?

12. Bus stop
How can people travel round the area?
Where do the buses go?

Key vocabulary

advertisement	houses	post box
building site	jobs	school
crossing	machines	shop
direction	map	sign
factory	play area	traffic

Copymasters
Use **Copymaster 36** (Street walk) to help children collect information about houses, places and street furniture in the local area.

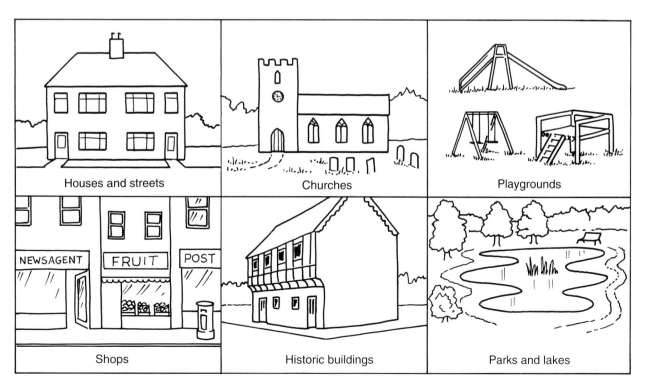

Houses and streets   Churches   Playgrounds

Shops   Historic buildings   Parks and lakes

31

VISITING A CHURCH

Most schools are within walking distance of a church. There is a wealth of things for children to see and do when they arrive. You can look at the patterns and decorations on the building, explore the graveyard and find out about the different plants and creatures that live there.

It is polite to contact the vicar before making the visit. If the church is kept locked up then you can arrange to collect the key. Churches are often the oldest buildings in the area and can be a rich source of historical evidence. It is also important that children understand they are special buildings which have a specific religious function.

Key vocabulary

altar	font	tiles
bells	nave	tombstone
brick	pulpit	tower
church	stained glass	weather vane
clock	stone	wood

Copymasters
Copymaster 37 (Inside a church) is a colouring sheet which will help to introduce children to the furniture and other special items in a church.

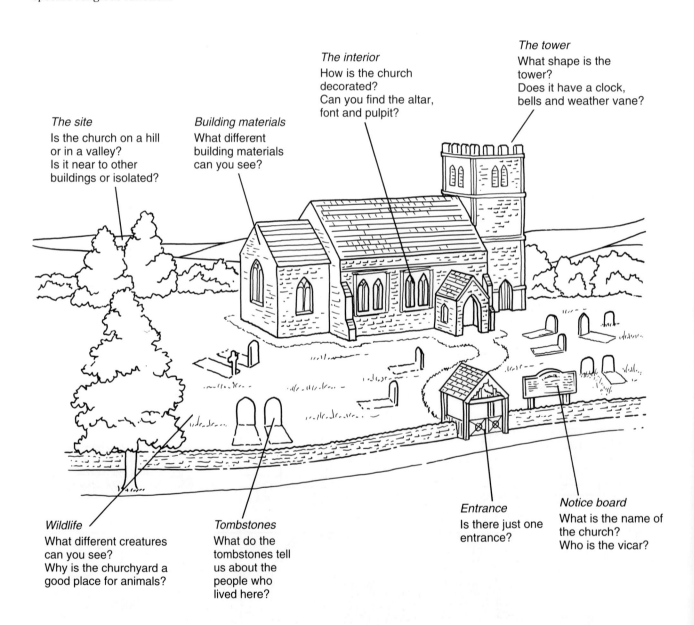

The interior
How is the church decorated?
Can you find the altar, font and pulpit?

The tower
What shape is the tower?
Does it have a clock, bells and weather vane?

The site
Is the church on a hill or in a valley?
Is it near to other buildings or isolated?

Building materials
What different building materials can you see?

Wildlife
What different creatures can you see?
Why is the churchyard a good place for animals?

Tombstones
What do the tombstones tell us about the people who lived here?

Entrance
Is there just one entrance?

Notice board
What is the name of the church?
Who is the vicar?

VISITING A SHOPPING PRECINCT

Shopping precincts are common features in towns and cities. They are designed to provide shoppers with a range of facilities which are easy to reach and attractive to use. The pedestrianised areas also allow people to relax and spend more time shopping.

There are plenty of things to discuss with the children. They could begin by looking at ways people reach the site and the things they can buy when they arrive. It is often instructive to look at the design. Street lamps, seats, decorations, plants and flowers all help to create a pleasant atmosphere.

Key vocabulary

car park	goods	safety
delivery area	lights	seats
entrance	litter bins	shops
facilities	paving	signs
flowers	precinct	toilets

Copymasters

Copymaster 38 (Going shopping) is designed to help children distinguish between different types of shop including bakers, newsagents and chemists.

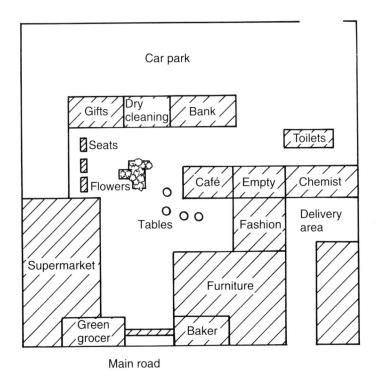

Are there enough parking spaces?

Is it easy to get in and out?

What facilities are there for the disabled?

What different shops can you find?

Can you buy everything you need here?

How are goods delivered to the shops?

Are there any empty shops?

What do you think any empty shops should be used for?

Is the shopping precinct busy with people?

How has the precinct been made attractive?

Look at the lights. They help to keep the precinct light and safe.

Look for places to sit. Seats encourage people to stay in the precinct.

Look for bright colours. They help to make people feel cheery.

Look for plants and flowers. They help to make people feel relaxed and enjoy shopping.

Look at the floor paving. Cars are not allowed into the precinct so people can walk where they like.

33

VISITING A BUS STATION

Young children are often fascinated by bus stations. There is plenty of coming and going. People hurry around as they set off on journeys. The buses provide a valuable service, linking together the town centre with the surrounding area.

You need to plan a visit to the bus station particularly carefully so that the children are not exposed to danger and keep out of the way of passengers. Try to arrange a talk with a member of staff so the children can ask questions about what happens. You might also take photographs to use when you get back to school.

Key vocabulary

bus	job	shed
cafe	journey	station
coach	office	telephone
fuel	passenger	ticket
garage	petrol	timetable

Copymasters

Use **Copymaster 39** (Bus game) to extend the work in a light-hearted way. The children will need a dice and counters and will need to work in pairs or small groups.

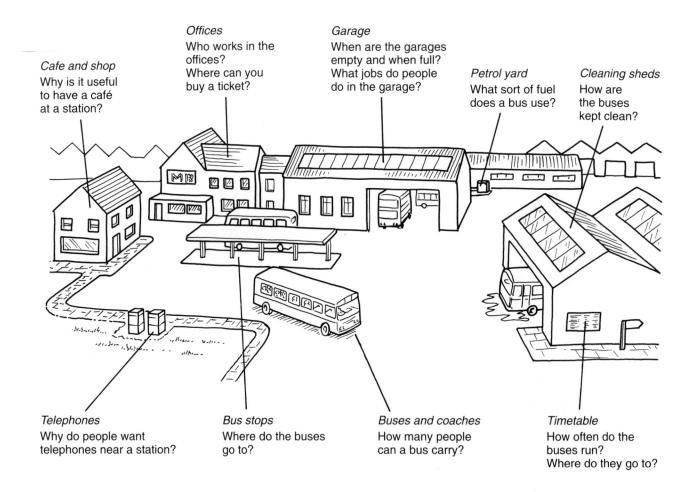

Cafe and shop
Why is it useful to have a café at a station?

Offices
Who works in the offices?
Where can you buy a ticket?

Garage
When are the garages empty and when full?
What jobs do people do in the garage?

Petrol yard
What sort of fuel does a bus use?

Cleaning sheds
How are the buses kept clean?

Telephones
Why do people want telephones near a station?

Bus stops
Where do the buses go to?

Buses and coaches
How many people can a bus carry?

Timetable
How often do the buses run?
Where do they go to?

34

VISITING A PARK

Parks are an established feature of the urban environment. They provide a place where people can go to relax and find peace and quiet. Most young children will be familiar with parks having visited them to look at the flowers and trees and use the play equipment. You can build on this experience as children explore their local environment.

From a practical point of view parks also have the advantage that they are safe places where children can work without fear of traffic dangers. However it is advisable to set very clear limits to how far the children can go. Otherwise they may respond to the feeling of freedom of space by scattering in different directions.

Key vocabulary

cafe	litter bins	seat
car park	park	sign
flower beds	path	soil
gate	play area	trees
grass	pond	visitors

Copymasters

Copymaster 40 (At the park I-spy) is an identification sheet which the children can use during a visit to the park.

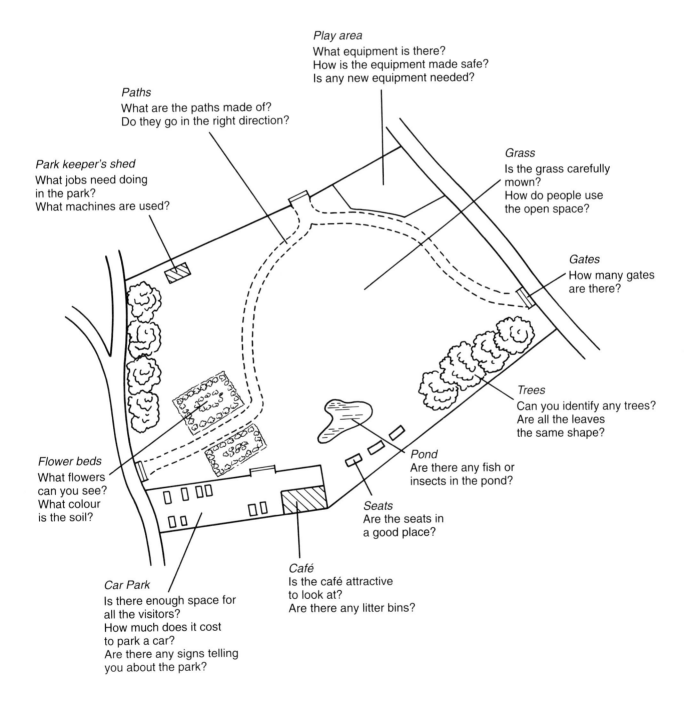

Play area
What equipment is there?
How is the equipment made safe?
Is any new equipment needed?

Paths
What are the paths made of?
Do they go in the right direction?

Park keeper's shed
What jobs need doing
in the park?
What machines are used?

Grass
Is the grass carefully mown?
How do people use the open space?

Gates
How many gates are there?

Trees
Can you identify any trees?
Are all the leaves the same shape?

Flower beds
What flowers can you see?
What colour is the soil?

Pond
Are there any fish or insects in the pond?

Seats
Are the seats in a good place?

Car Park
Is there enough space for all the visitors?
How much does it cost to park a car?
Are there any signs telling you about the park?

Café
Is the café attractive to look at?
Are there any litter bins?

35

VISITING A FARM

Farms have a romantic appeal to children. This is probably because farms are associated with animals and feature in stories. A farm visit can extend this interest and help them to understand more about their surroundings.

It is important that children realise farms produce food. Depending on the soil and climate, the land is either used for crops or grazing animals. There is a pattern of activities which varies with the seasons. As they visit the farmyard children will also see a range of equipment and machinery which will prompt discussion.

Key vocabulary

animal	gate	stream
countryside	hay	tractor
cow	machine	valley
farmyard	materials	wall
field	sheep	wood

Copymasters

Use **Copymaster 43** (On the farm) either to consolidate the work or as an assessment exercise to see if the children have learnt to recognise the different parts of a farm.

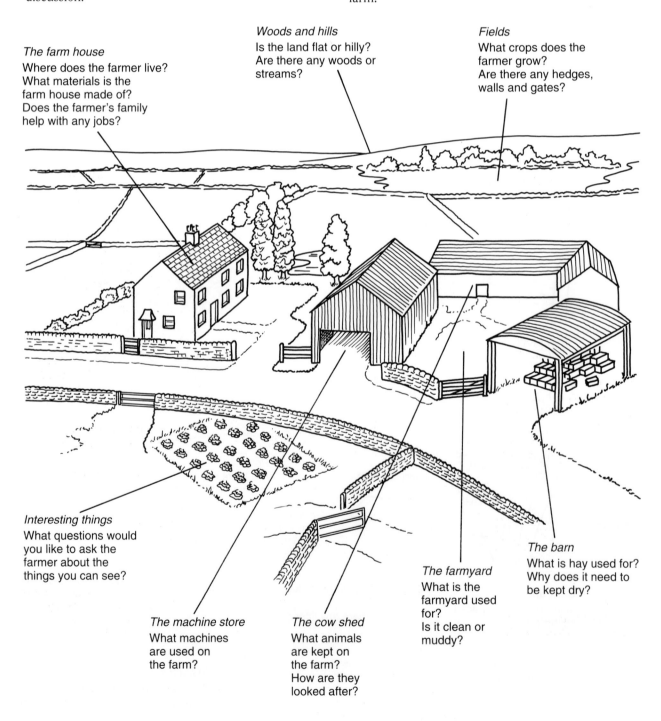

The farm house
Where does the farmer live?
What materials is the farm house made of?
Does the farmer's family help with any jobs?

Woods and hills
Is the land flat or hilly?
Are there any woods or streams?

Fields
What crops does the farmer grow?
Are there any hedges, walls and gates?

Interesting things
What questions would you like to ask the farmer about the things you can see?

The machine store
What machines are used on the farm?

The cow shed
What animals are kept on the farm?
How are they looked after?

The farmyard
What is the farmyard used for?
Is it clean or muddy?

The barn
What is hay used for?
Why does it need to be kept dry?

VISITING DIFFERENT ENVIRONMENTS

The land around us is used in a variety of different ways. In urban areas the local Council plans car parking spaces, play areas, parks and other recreational facilities. However, other areas are used in much more informal ways. Old factories and wasteground sites, for example, are often left empty for years before they are redeveloped. In the meantime they are colonised by plants and creatures.

There will be a variety of environments around most schools. If children visit some of these places and experience them for themselves it will help them to learn about the locality. It will also introduce them to the idea of land use, which is something that is explored at greater depth in Key Stages 2 and 3.

Key vocabulary

allotments	field	space
building site	playground	tidy
car park	pleasant	verge
change	recycling point	wasteground
environment	season	wood

Copymasters

As you explore different environments you may find it helpful to talk about how people look after their surroundings, using **Copymaster 42** (Caring for places).

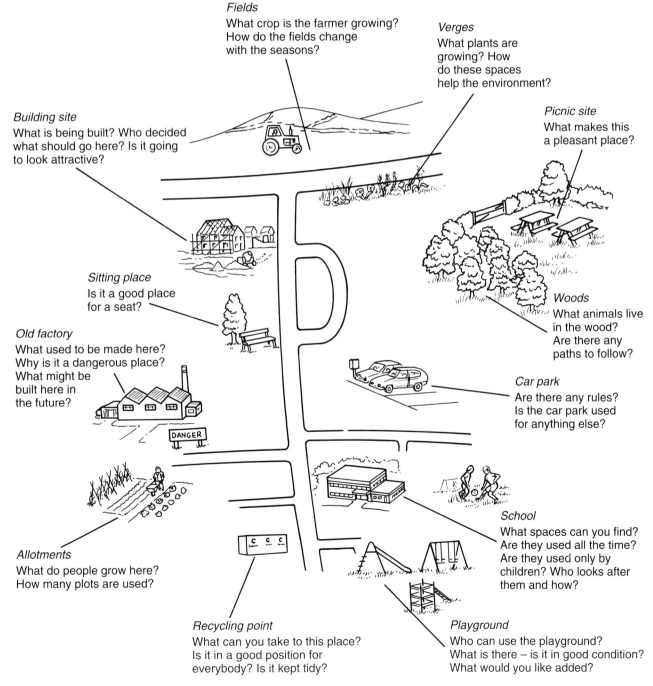

Fields
What crop is the farmer growing? How do the fields change with the seasons?

Verges
What plants are growing? How do these spaces help the environment?

Picnic site
What makes this a pleasant place?

Building site
What is being built? Who decided what should go here? Is it going to look attractive?

Sitting place
Is it a good place for a seat?

Woods
What animals live in the wood? Are there any paths to follow?

Old factory
What used to be made here? Why is it a dangerous place? What might be built here in the future?

DANGER

Car park
Are there any rules? Is the car park used for anything else?

School
What spaces can you find? Are they used all the time? Are they used only by children? Who looks after them and how?

Allotments
What do people grow here? How many plots are used?

Recycling point
What can you take to this place? Is it in a good position for everybody? Is it kept tidy?

Playground
Who can use the playground? What is there – is it in good condition? What would you like added?

37

A CONTRASTING LOCALITY

Two localities should be studied: the locality of the school and a locality either in the United Kingdom or overseas, in which the physical and/or human features contrast with those in the locality of the school. The locality of the school is its immediate vicinity; it includes the school buildings and grounds and the surrounding area within easy access. The contrasting locality should be an area of similar size.

Progression indicators
- name key features of a place they have studied
- consider what it would be like to live in the place they have studied
- compare the place they have studied with the local area

Interpretation
The children should find out about houses, jobs, landscape and environment in a village or small town.

Introduction
The relationship between people and the environment is a central idea in geography. Case studies, whether at a local, regional or national scale, are a powerful way of illustrating this connection. They show how people respond to their surroundings in everyday situations and give children a meaningful context in which to develop skills of mapwork, fieldwork and research.

When they study a contrasting locality, the children will need detailed information. It may prove possible to set up a link with a school in another part of the country and to exchange letters, tapes, photographs and maps. Alternatively, you could base the work on materials that you have assembled yourself, perhaps during a holiday or when visiting friends and relatives.

Two sample studies are included in this unit. The first concentrates on a rural community, using Broadwindsor in Dorset as an example. The second study focuses on Sandwich, a historic town on the coast of Kent. The maps, drawings and notes provide a range of material for the children to use.

There are considerable advantages if the children can visit the place they are studying and record information about it for themselves. There is no need to focus on distant locations. If you work in a suburban school, for example, you might be able to visit a local farm or village. In large conurbations you might compare one urban area with another. If you do decide to adopt this approach, the materials on Broadwindsor and Sandwich provide a format which you can follow.

Key vocabulary

bank	caravan
boat	castle
bridge	city
contrast	mine
difference	quarry
farm	site
fishing	toilet
harbour	tourist
historic	town
kiosk	village

Key questions
What is the place like?
How does it differ from your own place?
What are the natural things in the area?
How have people changed the area?

Picture books
Some picture books have a strong regional flavour, or may be relevant to a particular locality. *A Walk in the Park* by Anthony Browne (Hamilton, 1977) which is based on Greenwich Park is a case in point. With older children it may be appropriate to consider how the environment is changing. For example, *Shaker Lane* by Alice and Martin Provensen (Penguin, 1987) is about the effect of a new reservoir on an established community.

Activity 98 Contrasts

Materials needed
Pictures, photographs and maps of a contrasting locality.

Talk with the children about the features of the local area. What are the buildings and places which make it special? Now find out about a contrasting locality by looking at pictures, photographs, maps and other sources of information. In what way is it different from

Farm visit. The children can conduct their own interviews.

the place where you live? Record some of the key differences using **Copymaster 43** (Contrasts).

Activity 99 Fishing port

Materials needed
Maps, brochures, slides and souvenirs of a fishing port.

Provide the children with information about a fishing port. This might be somewhere you have visited on holiday. Alternatively, you could arrange for someone you know to describe a port to the children in an illustrated talk. How many fishing boats are there, and what fish do they catch? Is the place popular with visitors? Is there a natural harbour? Do storms cause damage in the winter? **Copymaster 44** (Fishing Port) will help to develop key vocabulary as well as setting the scene.

Slides are an excellent way of conveying geographical information.

Activity 100 Mining community

Materials needed
Leaflets and samples from a mining company. Maps and photographs of the surrounding area.

Write to a quarry or mining company for information about the work that they do. Enquire if they can send you a few samples of their products, along with pictures and brochures of their operations. Set up a display for the children to investigate. What is the name of the stone? What is it used for? How is it extracted? Put up a map of the mine and photographs of the places where the mine workers live. Talk with the children about the district. Any first-hand knowledge that you can contribute will be extremely valuable. Use **Copymaster 45** (Quarry) to support the work.

Activity 101 Tourist attraction

Materials needed
Tourist brochures and leaflets about a historic site, photographs, postcards and maps of the surrounding area.

Obtain brochures, leaflets and other promotional material about a tourist attraction such as an old abbey or castle. Where is it in relation to your own locality? Who lived there in the past, and why? How many people visit it nowadays? Provide the children with maps, postcards and photographs so that they can form an impression of the area. What clues are there that tourism is important for local people? As in Activity 100 (Mining community), your own personal knowledge will be important when the children come to make their investigations. **Copymaster 46** (Historic Site) provides some ideas which the children can pursue.

Activity 102 School link

Materials needed

Letters, maps, pictures, photographs, cassettes, models and other materials from a school in a contrasting area.

Set up a link with a school in a contrasting area. Arrange for them to send letters, maps, pictures, photographs, cassettes, models and other materials which convey an impression of their locality. Using this evidence, get the children to set up a display that highlights the contrast with the place where you live. You might ask the children a set of questions to help focus their attention. It will also be valuable to consider why places develop in different ways. The interplay between human and physical geography will then become apparent. **Copymaster 47** (City) illustrates some of the features of city environment and is designed to provide background information and vocabulary.

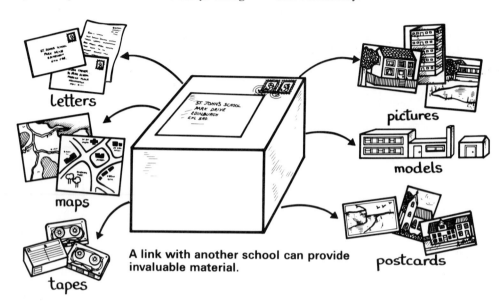

A link with another school can provide invaluable material.

Activity 103 Postcard corner

Materials needed

Postcards of places the children have visited, map of the United Kingdom.

Set up a display of postcards showing the places both you and the children have visited in the United Kingdom. Write a label under each one saying where it comes from. Include a map in the display. Give each postcard a number. Put the number next to the postcard and at the correct place on the map. You could extend the work by including a wider range of postcards, and talking about the distance to each of the different locations.

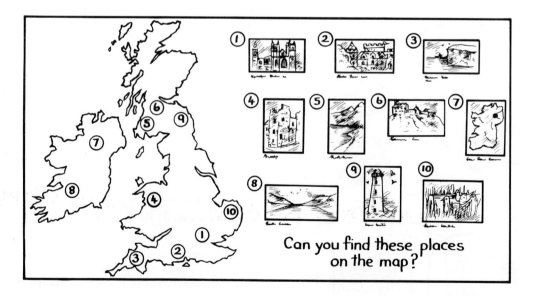

Can you find these places on the map?

Blueprints links

See the *Infant Geography Resource Bank* for case studies on Stevenage new town (copymasters 16 to 20) and Wembury, a seaside village near Plymouth (copymasters 11 to 15).

BROADWINDSOR, A VILLAGE IN DORSET

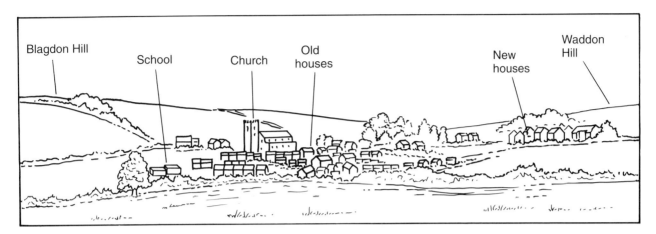

Broadwindsor is a small Dorset village. It is about 15 km inland from the coast, high in the hills to the north of Bridport.

The area is rich in history. The Romans set up their tents on nearby Waddon Hill during the invasion of Britain in AD 43. Many of the other hills in the district have Iron Age fortifications. The Ridgeway, parts of which are still visible a few kilometres to the south of the village, is even older. It dates back some 4,000 years and provided a route across southern Britain to East Anglia.

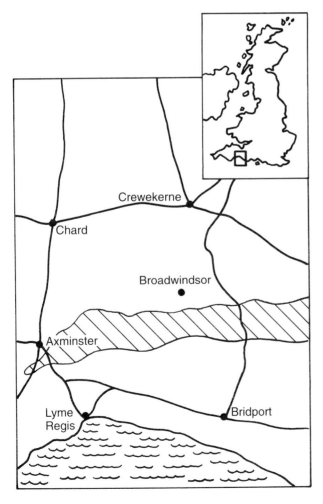

For centuries, Broadwindsor has served as the centre for an agricultural community. The census of trades for 1899 records 31 farmers, 8 shopkeepers, 7 innkeepers, 5 carpenters and a number of masons, shoe makers, saddlers and other artisans.

The population of the village grew from around 450 in 1662 to a peak of just under 1700 in 1841. Since then it has declined. Recently a considerable number of new houses has been put up. Some of these are rented out by a housing association.

One of the best accounts of Broadwindsor comes from the journals of Dorothy Wordsworth who lived in the area with her brother from 1795–1797.

'We have not the warmth and luxuriance of Devonshire, though there is no want either of wood or cultivation, but the trees appear to suffer from the sea blasts. We have hills, which, seen from a distance, almost take the character of mountains, some cultivated to their summits, others in their wild state. covered with furze and broom. . . . The greatest inconvenience we suffer here is in being so far from the post office . . .'

Broadwindsor has the five main components of a living village community.

- Church   Dates back to the eleventh century. Restored 1868.
- Church Hall   Provides a meeting place for local people.
- School   Present building opened in 1968. Nearly 90 children on role.
- Shops   General store supplies groceries. Separate Post Office.
- Pubs   The White Lion.

Copymasters

Copymasters 48–51 all focus on Broadwindsor and can be used in a variety of ways.

- Get the children to colour the sheets for a wall display.
- Blank out the captions on sheets 50 and 51 and ask the children to write the labels underneath the drawings.

41

THEME	QUESTION	ANSWERS
Landscape	What is the countryside like?	There is a range of hills between Broadwindsor and the coast. Wadden Hill is the site of a Roman camp and was used as a quarry for local stone. Lewesdon Hill is owned by the National Trust and is covered in beech and fir trees. Pilsdon Hill is an Iron Age Hill fort and one of the highest points in southern England (277 metres).
Weather	What is the weather like?	The climate is generally mild as the sea is not far away. However, the weather is frequently windy and rainfall is considerably higher than places further east.
Houses	Are all the houses the same?	The oldest houses are in the centre of the village. They are built of local sandstone. Originally the roofs were made of thatch but this has now been replaced by tiles. Between the Wars a few council houses were put up but most new development has occurred in the last thirty years.
Jobs	What jobs do people do?	Farming is still an important activity. There are a great variety of farms including dairying, sheep, pigs, vegetables and arable crops. Some people work in factories in the nearby towns. Others run small businesses such as house repairs, deliveries and household services. The area is popular for retirement and there is high percentage of old people.
Changes	How is Broadwindsor changing?	The number of houses in the village has doubled in recent years. A craft centre has opened in a converted farm complex. One of the two pubs has closed.

- Cut out the drawings of the buildings and use them to make a concertina book about Broadwindsor.
- Cut out the drawings of the people and buildings on sheets 50 and 51. Get the children to make a Venn diagram linking each person to the place where they work.

- Enlarge the map of Broadwindsor for a class display. You can do this by making a transparency from the copymaster and projecting it onto the wall using an OHP. The further you are from the wall the larger the projected image will become.

SANDWICH: A TOWN IN KENT

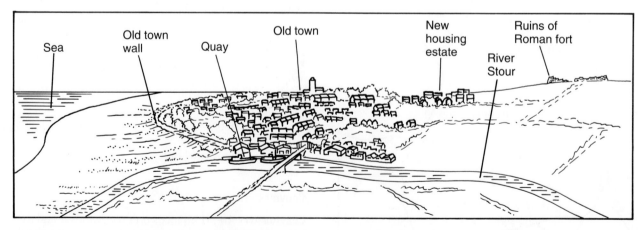

Sandwich is a small town on the coast of Kent. It was built by the Anglo-Saxons at the mouth of the River Stour close to the old fort at Richborough which had been the main point of entry to Roman Britain. It was originally called *Sandwic*, or the village on the sands.

In medieval times Sandwich was an important port. It handled wool and other goods that were exported to the continent. The town grew rich and churches and other fine buildings were put up.

Later, in the sixteenth century, large numbers of refugees from the Low Countries arrived in Sandwich to escape religious persecution. They set up a cloth-

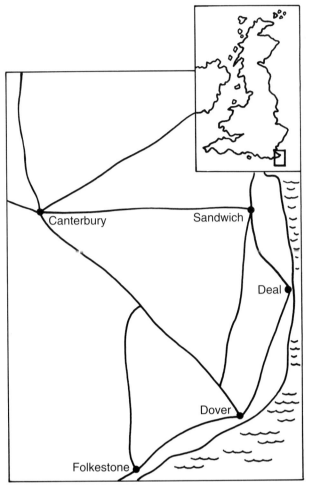

making industry. They also made use of the soil and the climate to establish market gardens. This was a significant innovation as the English were not used to eating vegetables at the time.

Nowadays Sandwich has a population of about 5,000 people. The estuary of the Stour has silted up and the town is now a couple of kilometres from the sea. The town centre has been preserved from development and retains much of its medieval fabric. Market gardening remains an important local industry. To the north of the town a large industrial complex has been established in the 'loop' of the Stour. This is dominated by Pfizer's, the international chemical company.

Sandwich has all the features of a small town.

- Churches   A number of different historic churches
- Schools   A primary and secondary school
- Shops   Food, clothes, furniture and other shops
- Market   A market square and guildhall
- Pubs   A number of inns and pubs including a hotel
- Factories   Factories which make electricity, medicines and machines
- Railway   A railway station with services to London

Copymasters
Copymasters 52–55 all focus on Sandwich and can be used in a variety of ways.

- Get the children to colour the sheets for a wall display.

THEME	QUESTION	ANSWERS
Landscape	What is the countryside like?	The countryside is almost completely flat, with very few trees. There are golf courses along the coast. Market gardens produce tomatoes, strawberries and other crops.
Weather	What is the weather like?	Sandwich is in one of the driest parts of the UK. It is also one of the sunniest. The sea tends to moderate temperatures, but the winds are stronger than average. This is one of the reasons an experimental wind turbine has been set up at the power station.
Houses	Are the houses all the same?	The town centre is full of ancient houses. The most historic are timber-framed but there are also large numbers of eighteenth century brick and painted cottages. New estates have been built on the edge of the town, particularly on the south east.
Jobs	What jobs do people do?	There is an industrial estate to the north of Sandwich on land which was used for a 'secret' munitions port in the First World War. A power station was built in the 1960s to use fuel from the Kent coalfield. Market gardening is an important activity in the surrounding countryside.
Changes	How is Sandwich changing?	There are plans for a large new supermarket on the edge of the town. This would have a big effect on the present shops. Pollution is a serious problem. The power station is burning a controversial new fuel, Orimulsion, which produces dirty, sulphurous smoke. Sandwich Bay is badly polluted with sewage. New, longer outfalls are being built but these may not prove effective. However, traffic levels have fallen considerably with the construction of a by-pass and this has improved the town centre a great deal.

- Blank out the captions on sheets 54 and 56 and ask the children to write labels underneath the drawings.
- Cut out the drawings for a concertina book about Sandwich.
- Enlarge the map of Sandwich for a class display. You can do this by making a transparency from the copymaster and projecting it onto the wall using an OHP. The further you are from the wall the larger the projected image will become.
- Use the drawings on sheet 55 to promote discussion about environmental issues. What are the problems and how are they each being solved?

AN OVERSEAS LOCALITY

Two localities should be studied: the locality of the school and a locality, either in the United Kingdom or overseas, in which the physical and/or human features contrast with those in the locality of the school. The locality of the school is its immediate vicinity; it includes the school buildings and grounds and the surrounding area within easy access. The contrasting locality should be an area of similar size.

Progression indicators
- name key features of a place they have studied
- consider what it would be like to live in the place they have studied
- compare the place they have studied with the local area

Interpretation
The children should find out about houses, jobs, landscape and environment in a village or small town in a country overseas.

Introduction
Young children often have curious and distorted ideas about the world beyond their local area. Nowadays most children have been to places outside the immediate vicinity, but even those who have travelled widely often only gain superficial images of different places.

This unit seeks to develop children's understanding of the wider world. It is important to note that the curriculum focuses attention on localities and small areas. However children are also expected to be aware of the broader geographical context at a regional or national scale. There is much to be said for concentrating on named families and everyday events. This will allow you to make comparisons with your own area, stressing similarities and common human needs.

The study of distant places is a relatively new and exciting dimension in the Key Stage 2 curriculum. It takes time to build up the necessary resources and expertise. Postcards, photographs, slides, artefacts, videos, first-hand accounts and stories are all valuable sources of information. There may also be opportunities for setting up direct links with a corresponding school so that the children can provide each other with first hand information.

Key vocabulary

clothes	language
country	people
environment	place
food	plants
holiday	travel
house	weather
journey	world

Key questions
In what way is the locality similar to your own?
In what way is it different?
What plants and animals live there?
What jobs do people do?
Is the environment changing?

Resources

Folk tales
Anthologies of folk tales are a good way of introducing a global dimension to your teaching. Older children may enjoy *Takkatoo's Journey* by Amanda Loverseed (Blackie, 1990) which is a beautifully illustrated Inuit tale.

Picture books
A variety of picture books are set in overseas locations. *A Nice Walk in the Jungle* by Nan Bodsworth (Kestrel, 1989) has vivid rainforest illustrations. *Percy Short and Cuthbert* by Susie Jenkin Pearce (Viking, 1990) involves a journey to the other side of the world. It offers excellent educational possibilities and should not be missed. *Jyoti's Journey* by Helen Ganley (André Deutsch, 1986) tells the story of an Indian girl who comes to live in England. *A Country Far Away* by Nigel Gray (Andersen, 1988) compares the life of a child in Africa with the life of a child in England.

Songs
'The World is Big, The World is Small', from *Tinderbox* (Black, 1982) is recommended.

Activity 104 Food from different places

Materials needed

Food labels, wool or cotton, world map.

Make a collection of labels from packets and tins. Look at them in turn and find out which foods come from the United Kingdom and which ones from other countries. Arrange the labels in a display around a map of the world. Fix lines of wool or cotton linking the labels to the correct countries.

Activity 105 Holidays

Materials needed

Posters, books and travel brochures, paint, paper.

Set up a display of posters, books and travel brochures showing different holiday destinations. Try to include as wide a range as possible, with cities, beaches, mountains, safari parks, and so on. Let the children select a holiday of their choice. Why did they choose it? What makes it special? Ask them to paint a picture of the place they would like to visit, and put up their work as part of a class display.

Activity 106 Looking at pictures

Materials needed

Photograph, picture or poster of an overseas locality.

Make a detailed study of a photograph or poster of an overseas locality. Talk with the children about what they can see, and how this compares with your own area. Pay particular attention to landforms, weather, plants and animals, buildings, transport and people at work. Write a list of the things that the children mention and put it up on the wall next to the picture, using the headings 'similar' and 'different'. You could ask the children to complete **Copymaster 56** (Looking at Pictures) and **Copymaster 57** (Similar or Different?).

Activity 107 Overseas communities

Are there any children in the class who were born abroad? Ask them to talk about their country of origin. What clothes do they wear there? What food do they eat? What are their houses like? Can they bring in books, pictures and objects for the class to look at? You may find that one of their parents is prepared to come and help with the project. Alternatively, there may be other teachers or helpers in the school who can contribute. Get the children to make drawings, listen to music, play games and perform simple dances illustrating aspects of the culture of the place they are studying.

Activity 108 Travellers

Invite someone who has lived or travelled in a foreign country to talk to the class. You may find that the children's parents or other members of staff will be able to put you in contact with a suitable person. Ideally they should know the place well and be able to describe it in some detail. It also helps if they have experience of talking to infants. Get the children to prepare their questions beforehand. They should try to find out about a wide range of topics such as food, clothes, customs, animals, weather and natural features.

Activity 109 Objects

Materials needed

Collection of objects from a locality overseas, photographs and books about the place chosen.

Talk with the children about the objects which give an impression of our lives. Make a list of a dozen key things. These should include clothes, toys, household objects, books and magazines. Now set up a display of objects from a locality overseas. You might obtain these yourself when on holiday. Another option is to set up a link with a school overseas, perhaps with the help of a local Development Education Group. Let the children sort the objects into groups and guess how they are used. What does each

Looking at pictures. Which features are similar and different to your own area?

45

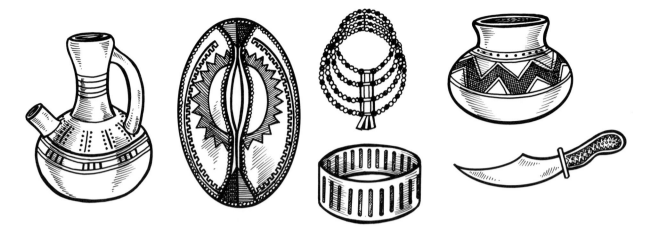

object indicate about the place that it comes from? Is it similar to or different from the things that we use? Get the children to make careful drawings of the objects. Books and reference material will help the children to find out more about the place where the objects originate.

Activity 110 Twinning

Materials needed

Maps, brochures and photographs of your twin town.

Find out from the local council if the place where you live is twinned with a community overseas. Many British towns have special associations with similar towns in France or Germany. See if you can arrange to borrow maps, brochures and photographs showing what your twin town is like. Is there anyone locally who has visited the place recently and who could give the children a first-hand account? See if it is possible to establish contact with a school in the area and to exchange information in a 'pen-pal' link. Organise a class project to explore the main similarities and differences. This could involve a great deal of cross-curricular work.

Activity 111 Buildings around the world

Materials needed

Photographs or pictures of buildings in different countries.

Give the children a collection of photographs or pictures of buildings around the world. Get them to sort them into places for living, places for working, places for worship, and so on. Discuss the differences that the children notice. Would they like to live in these buildings or visit them? Can they explain why they are different? Use the pictures on a number of different occasions, and get the children to sort them into sets using a variety of criteria, such as buildings from hot and cold lands, buildings for large and small numbers of people, buildings which look ugly and buildings which are attractive.

Activity 112 Symbols

Materials needed

Pictures or photographs of different places.

Put up some pictures or photographs or your locality and places overseas as a part of a wall display. Ask the children to colour and cut out the symbols in **Copymaster 58** (Symbols). They should then select the correct symbols for each picture and pin them underneath to complete the display. Talk about the pictures. In what ways is your own area different from other places? In what ways is it similar?

Activity 113 Soft toys

Materials needed
A collection of soft toy animals.

Ask the children to bring their soft toys to school. Put these out on display for the class to look at. How many of the creatures would be found in this country? How many come from abroad? Can the children think of any other way of sorting them into groups? Hot and cold places, and land and water provide some other possible divisions. Get the children to write labels for their toys, saying where they might come from. You could include a world map as part of the display and encourage the children to identify some of the main habitats, such as the icecaps and rainforests.

Activity 114 Television programmes

Materials needed
Schools' television programme about an overseas locality.

Show the children a schools' television programme about an overseas locality. There are an increasing number of programmes that provide portraits of life abroad. Use the programme as a stimulus for further work. For example, you might ask the children to make drawings and pictures for a concertina book about the place in the programme. You might also be able to broaden out the study to include more general information about the life and customs of the country.

Activity 115 Different scenes

Materials needed
General artwork materials.

Get the children to make a large class collage of a scene from another part of the world. This might be inspired by a visit from someone who has lived abroad, a television programme or a picture book. If your school is in a town or city the picture might show a country scene, or vice versa. Whatever you choose should prompt discussion and help to enlarge the children's view of the world.

Activity 116 Different languages

Materials needed
Labels, tickets, stamps, coins and books in European languages, a map of Europe.

Make a display of labels, tickets, stamps, coins and books written in European languages. Discuss the different European languages with the class. Do any of the children know a foreign language? Can they say a few foreign words which they can translate into English? Talk about where each language is spoken, using a map of Europe.

Activity 117 World music

Materials needed
Tape recorder, cassettes of music from around the world.

Introduce the children to traditional music from different parts of the world. You will need a tape recorder and a selection of cassettes. Your local library may be able to help. Play the children some suitable extracts and talk about the differences in the style of the music. Is the music joyful or sad? When do you think it might be played? What images does it conjure up?

Blueprints links
The *Infant Geography Resource Bank* contains a study of Chinon in France (copymasters 21–25). The town is on the banks of a tributary of the Loire in western France and is in the heart of a wine-making area.

RESOURCES ON OVERSEAS LOCALITIES

When you select a contrasting overseas locality you need to consider how you can obtain information. If you have visited the place yourself and can provide first hand accounts and materials for the children to study, that will be ideal. Direct links between schools also have great potential. Alternatively you may decide to use published resources. Many of these contain excellent photographs as well as maps, diagrams and supporting notes.

General materials
World Watch Themes Pack (Collins, 1993). Forty-eight stunning laminated A3-size colour photographs of scenes from the UK and around the world.
Ginn Geography Big Book (Ginn, 1991). Pictures, photographs, maps and plans of the UK and other parts of the world.
Oliver and Boyd Geography (Oliver and Boyd, 1991–5).

A set of booklets on themes and localities for Key Stage 1 as well as a large picture resource book.

Time and Place (Simon and Schuster, 1992). A set of boxes containing pictures, activities and games on history and geography.

Atlases

Keystart First Atlas (Collins-Longman, 1991). Introduces maps and plans at a variety of scales from the global to the local.

Oxford Infant Atlas (Oxford, 1991). Contains clear and simple world maps.

Locality packs

The overseas locality packs currently available are all aimed at Key Stage 2. However, they usually contain photographs and can be adapted and modified for use with younger children.

1. *Focus on Castries, St Lucia* (Geographical Association). Includes 28 A4-size full-colour photographs and background information.
2. *Lima lives* (Save the Children). A photo pack which explores the lives of some of the people who live in different parts of the city of Lima in Peru.
3. *Pampagrande* (Action Aid). A locality study pack focusing on a village in the Peruvian Andes. Contains 32 A4 colour photographs.
4. *Where Camels Are Better Than Cars* (Save the Children) Everyday life in Douentza, a market town in Mali, as seen through the eyes of four different people.
5. *My Village – Ilesha* (Worldaware). A portrait of a Nigerian village, Ilesha. Teaching materials include two posters and a specially-written story.
6. *Eritrea – Africa's newest country* (Christian Aid). Daily life, food, farming, weather and culture of two families in two localities in Eritrea. Includes 28 photographs.
7. *Nairobi – Kenyan City Life* (Action Aid). Thirty A4 colour photographs, maps and notes about life in a slum area of a major African city.
8. *Kapsokwony Rural Kenya* (Action Aid). A photo-based activity pack about the village of Kapsokwony in western Kenya. Focuses on the Wanyonyi family and their farm.
9. *Palm Grove* (UNICEF). Photographs, information and a poster about the contrasting life styles of people who live around Palm Grove Basic School, Victoria Falls, Zambia.
10. *Change in the Swat Valley – Pakistan* (Action Aid). A locality case study investigating the changes taking place in a traditional rural community. Complements the BBC *Landmarks* series.
11. *Ladakh* (Geographical Association). A study of a school and a Tibetan children's village in Ladakh, northern India. Contains 28 A4 colour photographs together with descriptions and supporting activities.
12. *Chembakoli – A Village in India* (Action Aid). One of the first and most popular of all the locality study packs. Photographs, maps and notes provide information about different aspects of life in a south Indian village.

Stories

The Farmer, the Leopard and the Hare (Action Aid). An illustrated collection of seventeen traditional short stories from around the world.

Under the Mango Tree (Longman). Two lively books with a selection of traditional poems and rhymes from Africa.

Tales from the Caribbean (Ginn). Set of four books on traditional stories and poems with suggestions for teaching activities.

Stories from Overseas (Oxfam). Illustrated booklets of stories for 5–9 year olds from Africa and south Asia.

Note: Most of the stories and locality packs listed above can be obtained from Oxfam, Worldaware or the Development Education Centre (Birmingham).

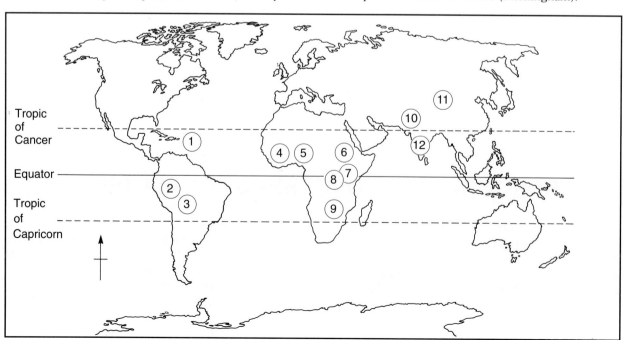

THEMES

THEMATIC STUDY

■ **6.** The quality of the environment in any locality, either in the United Kingdom or overseas, should be investigated.

In this study, pupils should be taught:

a to express views on the attractive and unattractive features, *eg tidiness, noise*, of the environment concerned, *eg a play area, a street, a small area of woodland*;

b how that environment is changing, *eg increasing traffic*;

c how the quality of that environment can be sustained and improved, *eg creating cycle lanes, excluding cars from an area.*

As well as studying places and learning geographical skills, children should be introduced to themes as part of their work. Themes bring together different aspects of geography and allow children to make links and connections. At Key Stage 2 only one theme is specified – the quality of the environment. This retains the balance of the previous Orders in which the environment appeared as a separate Attainment Target.

There are plenty of opportunities for practical work. On a personal level you can encourage children to use resources wisely and conserve energy. On a more general level you can conduct investigations in the school building and immediate surroundings.

It is important to consider ways of solving problems so that the children are not left with the impression that there is nothing they can do. Our individual actions can and do have an enormous impact, and groups such as Greenpeace and Friends of the Earth have shown what can be achieved through determined action.

This section also considers a number of other geographical themes, namely houses, shops, jobs, journeys, water, materials and weather. Although these themes are not specifically mentioned in the curriculum Orders, many schools work through common topics at Key Stage 1 and will want to combine geography with other subjects. The activities that are suggested show the potential of an inter-disciplinary approach.

ENVIRONMENT

BACKGROUND INFORMATION FOR THE TEACHER ▶

Facts and figures

● Half the rubbish we throw away could be recycled.

● A car produces approximately four times its own weight of carbon dioxide a year.

● World population is increasing by over a million people each week.

● Half of the world's plants and animals could become extinct in the next sixty years.

● By the middle of the next century world temperatures are expected to rise by between 1.5 and 4.5°C.

The environmental crisis is a relatively new phenomenon. It has been prompted partly by the development of industry and technology, and partly by the sheer growth of the human population. In the last 40 years manufacturing industry has increased sevenfold and world population has approximately doubled. This has put the environment under more and more stress.

Natural resources
The problem is compounded by the unequal distribution of resources. The world's richest nations,

North America, Europe, Japan and Australiasia, possess nearly all the world's wealth and are responsible for creating most of the pollution. By contrast, many people in Africa, southern Asia and Latin America live in great poverty and are forced to exploit the environment in order to survive.

Vulnerable environments
Many experts agree that the next decade will be critical as far as the environment is concerned. Acid

rain, nuclear radiation, desertification and the clearance of the rainforests are some of the issues which are hitting the headlines on an almost daily basis. The most serious threat of all is perhaps the prospect of irreversible climate change caused by greenhouse gases. It is, however, in the nature of environmental problems that they are all inter-related.

Managing the environment
There are many different things we can do to tackle the problems. Greater social justice, more efficient use of resources, recycling and sustainable development all offer encouraging possibilities. Children and adults alike need to be well informed so that they can make sensible choices and play their part in fashioning responsible attitudes.

ATTRACTIVE AND UNATTRACTIVE FEATURES ▶

The quality of the environment, in any locality, either in the United Kingdom or overseas, should be investigated. In this study, pupils should be taught to express views on the attractive and unattractive features, *eg tidiness, noise,* of the environment concerned, *eg a play area, a street, a small area of woodland.*

Progression indicators
- talk about safe and dangerous places
- describe attractive and unattractive places
- give reasons for their feelings about places

Interpretation
The children should talk about the things they like and dislike in the local area or some other place using terms such as 'noisy', 'quiet', 'dull', 'interesting', 'ugly' and 'beautiful'.

Introduction
The quality of the environment is fundamental to our standard of living. People are becoming increasingly aware of the threats to the natural world, and are seeking ways to protect it for the future. This unit focuses on the children's subjective response and asks them to consider what they like and dislike in their surroundings.

The idea is deceptively simple. Ideally, children should be encouraged to give reasons for their opinions, not to make snap judgements. They should also appreciate that other people think differently about the same things. These are heavy demands for infants.

One of the best approaches is to develop basic descriptive vocabulary. Children can be encouraged to consider the physical environment by talking about rivers, hills, parks, and other landscape features. If the children are given a chance to work in groups, this will help them to develop a balanced viewpoint. Whatever approach you adopt, remember to respect individual sensibilities if the streets and homes where children live are considered in any of the work that you organise.

Key vocabulary

beautiful	people
damage	place
dislike	quiet
dull	smelly
interesting	smoky
like	spoil
litter	tidy
noisy	ugly

Key questions
What do you like and dislike about your school? Why?
Are the things you like always good?
Are the things you dislike always bad?
What can you do about the things you dislike?

Resources

Folk tales
'The Fisherman and his Wife' by the Brothers Grimm is a powerful story of greed which raises questions about how we respond to our surroundings. You could use it as a way of getting the children to talk about what they like and dislike.

Picture books
The contrast between urban and rural environments is explored in the well-known story of the town mouse and the country mouse. There are a number of picture-book versions including *The Town Mouse and the Country Mouse* by Paul Galdone (Bodley, 1971). *The Tale of Johnny Town Mouse* by Beatrix Potter considers the same theme in a different way and concludes 'one place suits one person, another place suits another person'. Another delightful picture book is Brian Wildsmith's *Daisy* (Oxford, 1984). This tells the story of Daisy the cow who escapes from her field and goes to see the world, but decides that her own environment is best after all.

Activity 118 Things we like in school
Get the children to make a list of all the things they like about their class and school. Ask them to make

POLISH SMELL

like   dislike

6 children liked the smell
of polish in the hall.
3 children disliked it.

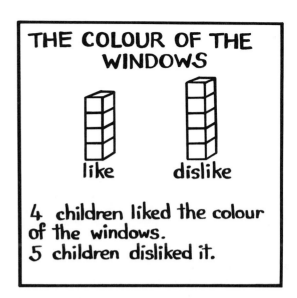

THE COLOUR OF THE WINDOWS

like   dislike

4 children liked the colour
of the windows.
5 children disliked it.

drawings of some of their favourite things. Mount the drawings in a class book with sentences under each one explaining what is good about it.

Activity 119 Sensory walk

Plan a sensory walk around the school. What unpleasant sounds and smells do the children notice? What things do they like the feel of? You could use **Copymaster 59** (Smells I Don't Like), **Copymaster 60** (Sounds I Don't Like) and **Copymaster 61** (Things I Like to Touch) to record the information. Alternatively, you could get the children to express their opinions by voting for individual items. For example, how many children like the smell of polish in the hall? How many dislike it? The information from the survey can be displayed as a simple block graph. Unifix blocks are ideal for this purpose and can lead to further work on a computer.

Activity 120 Word game

Materials needed

Set of flash cards, Blu-Tack.

Make a set of flash cards using the words from **Copymaster 62** (Word Game). Teach the children how to read the words using the flash card technique. Then give each child the copymaster sheet and ask them to

Word game. The children pin their words to different items.

make their own set of word cards. Play the Word Game, getting the children to express their likes and dislikes of eight items in the class or school by fixing the cards to them using Blu-Tack. You will need to agree with the children what items they are going to select, and explain that the cards must be placed face down so that the word is not visible. The children are allowed to put their cards in the same place as each other's, as long as they do not overlap.

When all the cards have been used up, you should turn them over while the children watch. Do all the cards say the same thing? Make a list of the objects selected, and record if they are mostly liked, mostly disliked, or both liked and disliked.

Activity 121 The local environment
Go for a sensory walk in the local environment. What smells, sounds, sight and surfaces do the children like and dislike? Use **Copymaster 63** (Different Environments) to record this information. Could anything be done to improve the places which are generally disliked? How would the children introduce more of the things that they like? Choose some of the best ideas, get the children to illustrate them, and send their suggestions off to the local council Planning Department.

Activity 122 Different features
Make a list of all the features which the children generally think make something likeable. You might consider colour, shape, texture, perfume, natural sounds, and so on. Using this list, test the school and locality to see how these features are used. Are there any obvious gaps or omissions? How do the children think the environment might be improved?

Activity 123 Different opinions
Materials needed
Outline plan of the school.

Ask the children to design two different signs. One should say 'I like this place', the other should say 'I dislike this place'. Place the signs on your plan of the school.

Ask other people what they think. You might invite the headteacher, the caretaker, a parent or visitor to give their views. Record the different opinions on a table or chart.

Consider the places a bird, mouse, spider and other creatures would like in and around your school. What are the things they would want in their ideal environment? Draw pictures of different creatures with dream bubbles showing their favourite place. Add a sentence underneath describing what each picture shows.

Activity 124 Likes and dislikes
Materials needed
Artwork materials.

Ask the children to paint a picture or draw a map of their journey to school. Discuss the things they like on the route. Do they pass any places they dislike? Make a list using a table with two columns with the headings 'likes' and 'dislikes'. Make a display of the pictures and maps and add the lists underneath.

Activity 125 Good for children
Materials needed
Artwork materials, map of your local area.

Talk about places in the locality which are good for children. Which places are dangerous? Get the children to do drawings of as many places, safe and unsafe as they can think of. If they think the place is dangerous they should put a red circle round the drawing. If they think it is safe they should put a blue rectangle round the edge. Arrange the drawings around a map of the locality and add the heading 'Safe and Dangerous Places'.

Different opinions. What makes an ideal environment?

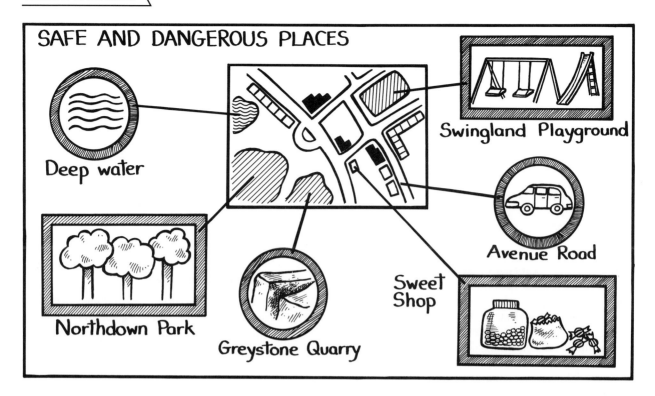

SAFE AND DANGEROUS PLACES

Deep water

Swingland Playground

Northdown Park

Greystone Quarry

Sweet Shop

Avenue Road

Activity 126 A far-away place

Materials needed
Postcards, pictures and photographs of a distant place.

Get the children to look at postcards and pictures of a place beyond their locality. Discuss what they like and dislike about each one. You might have a checklist of questions covering the physical features, buildings and settlements, and the quality of the environment. If possible, arrange for someone who has been to this place to come and talk to the children. Are they able to confirm or deny what the children have deduced from the pictures? What did they like and dislike about the place?

Blueprints links
You could use sheets 1–9 in the *Infant Geography Resource Bank* to get the children to talk about and compare different types of environment from a small village to a large city.

CHANGES IN THE ENVIRONMENT

The quality of the environment, in any locality, either in the United Kingdom or overseas, should be investigated. In this study, pupils should be taught how that environment is changing, *eg increasing traffic*.

Progression indicators
● understand that people do different activities on different days of the week
● talk about changes at home and in the immediate surroundings
● understand changes in a human lifetime

Interpretation
The children should be taught about how the environment is changing as farms are altered, new roads and houses are built and pollution and conservation affect our surroundings.

Introduction
Human activity has had an enormous impact on the environment. For centuries people have struggled to eke out a living from the land, and competed against the elements for survival. Modern technology has changed all this. We now have unprecedented power to alter the world for our own ends. With this power comes new responsibilities.

Children tend to believe that the world into which they have been born has always been the same. They need to be introduced to the idea that at one time in the past all places were countryside. It is hard even for adults to imagine that large cities and towns are a relatively recent phenomenon. Young children can only be expected to develop a piecemeal understanding of how people have changed their surroundings.

One of the best ways of introducing this unit is to consider the changes which have affected the children in their own lifetime. Examples might include moving house, changes in the garden, the acquisition of pets, a new baby in the family, and so on. The children could then discuss small-scale changes to their environment. You could group these into different categories, such as new roads and buildings, changes in the countryside, pollution and conservation. Depending on the age and ability of the children, you might decide to extend the discussion to cover a greater timescale and thereby enlarge their understanding of environmental change.

Key vocabulary

buildings	fumes	pollution
change	litter	road
country	nature	surroundings
environment	park	world
farm	people	

Key questions

How old is it?
What was there before?
How have my home and school changed?
Who causes these changes?
What changes happen very slowly?
What changes happen very quickly?

Resources

Picture books

In the last few years there has been a spate of excellent picture books on pollution and environmental themes. These include: *Oi! Get off our Train* by John Burningham (Cape, 1989), *The World that Jack built* by Ruth Brown (Andersen, 1990), *Rainforest* by Helen Coucher (Deutsch, 1988), *One World* by Michael Foreman (Andersen, 1990).

Songs

'Air', 'Leave Them a Flower' and 'Across the Hills' are some of the songs about pollution in *The Jolly Herring* by Roger Bush (A & C Black, 1980).

Activity 127 Things which change

Working as a class, make a list of different things which change. Examples might include the weather, day and night, plants, animals and people. Display the list and get the children to make drawings of some of the things they have mentioned. **Copymaster 64** (Things which Change) will help to develop this activity.

Activity 128 Change dial

Materials needed

Circles of card, scissors, glue, split pins.

Using **Copymaster 65** (Change Dial), get the children to make a series of 'before' and 'after' pictures of something that changes. They should then mount their pictures on a circular piece of card. Cut a window or opening in a second piece of card large enough to reveal just one of the pictures at a time. Assemble the two pieces with a split pin in the centre and ask the children to write the word 'change' on the front.

Activity 129 Farms and factories

Materials needed

Toy vehicles, animals and buildings, posters and pictures of farms and factories.

Collect posters and pictures which show farm and factory scenes. Ask the children to bring in toys which relate to these pictures and make some model farm and factory buildings. When you have assembled a reasonable collection, set up a display table showing farming activities. Change the display each day by taking away one or two farm items and replacing them with industrial buildings and vehicles. By the end of a week the display should be almost, but not quite, covered with factories. Talk about the changes as they happen. Get the children to make a diary, or draw simple plans and pictures, of the different scenes. Can any children think of places nearby where something similar has happened? Reinforce the work using **Copymaster 66** (Spot the Difference).

Activity 130 Change in your local area

Materials needed

Old photographs and postcards of the place where you live, simple maps and plans.

Make a collection of old photographs and postcards of the place where you live. Ask the children to bring in pictures which their parents or grandparents have collected. Find out if there are any books with collections of historic photographs of your area. Have any been reproduced in local newspapers? Put the pictures up as a display and link them to a street plan or map. See if you can find any old maps showing how your settlement has grown. Ask elderly people to come and see your exhibition and talk about what they remember from the past. Dress for a day in Victorian costume. Talk about things which would have been different in those times. Would your school have existed? How many local buildings would have been built? Make pictures of some different scenes from the past.

Activity 131 Obsolete objects

Materials needed

A range of obsolete items and their modern equivalents.

Make a display of objects which are old-fashioned or obsolete. Talk about each one with the children. What was it used for? How was it used? Why is it no longer

Drawing of change mounted on card

Card circle with 'window'

split pin

Change dial

needed? Try to group the items together. For example, all the things which were used in the home could be put into one area, while tools and equipment for workmen could be put into another. Talk about the modern equivalents for each item and add them to your display if possible. How many things used to be worked by hand but are now powered by electricity? Make a survey of electrical goods in school. Where are the sockets? How does the electricity get from place to place? Talk about where electricity comes from, the impact of power lines on the environment and the problems that power stations cause.

Activity 132 New things
Materials needed
Sticky paper, scissors.

Go for a walk around your school. Try to decide what has changed recently. Are there any new displays? Which books have been added to the library? Have any repairs been done? This exercise is a useful way of developing the children's observational skills and it illustrates how the school environment is always changing. You could get the children to cut out some

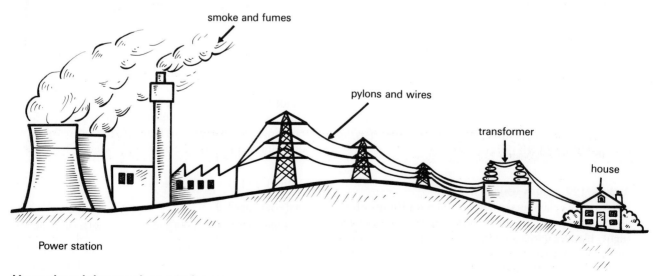

Power station

How electricity reaches our homes

stickers or stars to fix on to the things they have discovered. Back in the classroom they could make a list of all the things they remember.

sticky paper

Activity 133 Door walk
Materials needed
Rectangles of white card, artwork materials.

Go for a walk around some local streets to look at front doors. In what ways are they different? Why do people replace their front doors? Which ones look best? Give the children some rectangles of white card and ask them to design a front door of their own. Alternatively, you could use **Copymaster 67** (Front Doors) to make a frieze. Get the children to look at the school front door. How does it contribute to the appearance of the building? Could it be improved in any way?

Activity 134 Advertisements
Make a survey of advertisements in your local area. Where can you find them? Plan a walk linking together advertisements in shop windows and on hoardings, walls and lamp posts. What different things are advertised? Do advertisements spoil the view, or do they hide a messy place? What advertisements are there in your school? Have they been there a long time, and do they need replacing?

Activity 135 Favourite building
Materials needed
Clipboards, drawing paper, camera, binoculars.

Discuss different buildings near your school with the children, and choose one which they like. Organise a short outing to visit and study it in detail. Get the children to make drawings of the building from different angles. See that they look especially closely at the windows, doors, roof and decorations. You could take a pair of binoculars to help them make out the details. Photographs can also help to record information and are useful in any class display. Discuss how the building contributes to the environment. What would the children feel if someone decided to knock it down? Get the class to design and draw some buildings of their own. What sort of place would they put them in? Would they be suitable for a hill top, a valley, a large open space or a city high street?

Activity 136 Wear and tear
Materials needed
Card, scissors.

Examine the school buildings and grounds to look for examples of wear and tear. Examples might include flaking paintwork, broken roof tiles, cracks in the wall, trampled grass, worn verges and scratched brickwork. Help the children to spot these different things by making a simple 'looking eye' from card. When you get back to the classroom ask the children to write a sentence about each one. You could mount their work with the looking eye over the top like a frame. Discuss what has caused the damage.

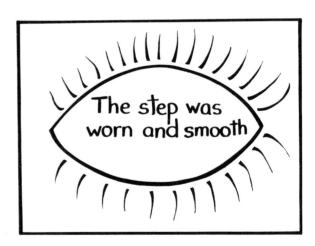

'Looking eye' made from card

► IMPROVING THE ENVIRONMENT ►

The quality of the environment in any locality, either in the United Kingdom or overseas, should be investigated. In this study, pupils should be taught how the quality of that environment can be sustained and improved, *eg creating cycle lanes, excluding cars from an area.*

Progression indicators
- talk about changes and improvements at home and school
- describe how the school might be improved
- compare two schemes for the same place

Interpretation

If possible, the children should undertake a practical activity. This might involve a school improvement project, such as setting up a garden or nature area. Alternatively, the children could be involved in a scheme to collect waste paper or steel or aluminium drink cans for recycling.

Introduction

Young children are often surprisingly knowlegeable about environmental issues. They receive information about current affairs from the television, radio and other media sources. Some children may have direct experiences of helping in a simple recycling project or conservation scheme. By the time they come to school quite a few children will have gathered a wide variety of information.

This unit builds on and extends children's interest. It considers the ways in which places can be improved. Children need to realise that what they do does have an effect on the world, and that they can do something positive.

One way of illustrating this idea is to talk about places that children are allowed to visit around school and the things they are allowed to do. Are there any rules governing their behaviour? How could other children spoil their enjoyment? You could then proceed to investigate different habitats around the school and think about possible improvements.

Key vocabulary

animal	improve
attractive	nature
beautiful	plants
bird	playground
earth	recycle
environment	school
garden	surroundings
habitat	wildlife

Key questions

What are you allowed to do?
What are you not allowed to do?
How could you improve your environment?
Which grown-ups help to improve the environment?
What do they do?

Resources

Picture books

The Hurricane Tree by Libby Purves (Bodley, 1988) tells the story of what happened in the hurricane of October 1987, and how the damage was repaired. *Nowhere to Play* by Kurusa (Black, 1981) is another true story. It describes how children struggled to find a playground in a South American city. For a more light-hearted approach you might read the children 'A House is Built for Eeyore at Pooh Corner' from *The House at Pooh Corner* by A.A. Milne.

Rhyme

Mary, Mary, Quite Contrary

'Mary, Mary, quite contrary,
How does your garden grow?'
'With silver bells and cockle shells,
And pretty maids all in a row'.

Activity 137 Classroom improvements

Materials needed
Home improvement magazines, furniture catalogues, samples of wallpaper and curtain materials.

Ask the children how they would redesign or redecorate the classroom. What colours would they use for the paintwork? Would they add a carpet or wallpaper? What style of furniture would they choose? Make up an 'improvements book' with samples of materials, advertisements for paint types and pictures from furniture catalogues.

Activity 138 School improvements

Materials needed
Simple plan of the school.

Explore your school with the class and decide on any changes they would make. Make a list of ideas using the headings: 'new paint', 'carpets', 'flowers' and 'pictures'. Using **Copymaster 68** (School Improvements), get the children to make signs to place around the school at the places they have selected. Give each sign a code and plot it on a simple outline map of the school. Get the children to explain each idea in greater detail in an accompanying 'improvements manual' as a follow-up exercise. (Further ideas on the school improvements theme are suggested in Activity 139).

Activity 139 Dream ideas

Materials needed
Class display book, photographs of individual children.

Many of the ideas which the children will suggest for improvements are likely to be rather unrealistic. You could make a collection of these suggestions in a book of dream ideas. Examples might include a sweet shop in the playground or a time travel capsule. If you add a drawing or a small photograph of the child next to each suggestion it will help to give the book a distinctive identity.

Activity 140 Plans for the future

Arrange for the headteacher or chairperson of the governors to visit the class and talk about what they

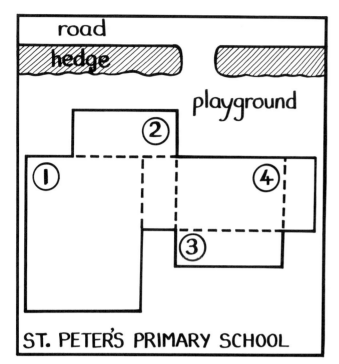

Plans for the future. Improvements manual

would like to do to improve the school. Are there big and small projects? What could be done soon, and what will take many years to achieve? Is there anything which could be done at no cost at all? Will outsiders be needed to help make the improvements? How can the children help?

Activity 141 The outside view
Look at two different views of your school. Using **Copymaster 69** (Different Views), get the children to decide which view they prefer. Discuss how they would improve the view they do not like. What are the things which spoil it? What could be added to create interest? Would it be possible to add colour or vegetation? Get the children to make paintings of the improvements they would like to see made.

Activity 142 Wildlife area

Materials needed

Logs, stones, flower pots, old bricks, dustbin lid.

Improve the environment for small creatures by building a wildlife area. Find a suitable place in the school grounds and count the number of creatures you can find. Record the results on **Copymaster 70** (Wildlife Survey). Add some stones, logs, flower pots on their side and old bricks with gaps in between them. If possible, include an upturned dustbin lid. Keep watch on the area and make a survey of the wildlife at suitable intervals, such as once a week or a month. What changes do you notice? Does your project appear to have benefited wildlife?

Activity 143 Tree planting

Materials needed

Cardboard, gardening sticks, Sellotape.

Take a careful look at the school grounds and decide where it might be useful to plant some new trees. Get the children to make some cardboard cut-out trees

using a template. Fix the trees to gardening sticks with glue or sellotape and 'plant' them in the places the children have selected.

Activity 144 Recycling scheme
Set up a recycling scheme for waste paper or aluminium cans. Establish a collecting point somewhere in the classroom and record the amount of material brought in each day. You could weigh the amount of paper or count the number of cans and show the results on a bar chart. Arrange for the material to be collected after a month or at the end of term. How much money has it raised? What will it be spent on? Find out about the recycling process from reference books and discuss what other materials can be used again. **Copymaster 71** (Recycling) is designed to help children record their ideas.

Activity 145 Improvements in the local area
Go for a walk in your local area and note down any improvements that you notice. Look for new doors, windows, garages and driveways. Are there any new signs, paths or play equipment in the local park? What are people doing to look after the environment? Discuss ways in which further improvements might be made and write to the local council planning department with your ideas.

Activity 146 Working for the environment
Make a list of people who work to improve or look after the environment. Examples include painters and decorators, builders, gardeners, architects and designers. Think also about people who work to improve conditions for poor people, either in this country or abroad. Some children may have heard of agencies such as Oxfam and Save the Children. Find out about environmental organisations such as Greenpeace and Friends of the Earth. What do they do? Write to them and ask them to send leaflets and information for the children to study. Why is their work important?

OTHER THEMES

The themes in this section group together material in the geography curriculum in a way which is appropriate for young children. They may prove particularly useful to Welsh schools where the geography Orders offer a choice between topics on the weather, jobs, journeys and the environment. However they also relate directly to the integrated topics which are followed by many infant schools throughout the UK.

Houses

Until about 1850, most houses in this country were built of local materials according to local craft traditions. With the coming of the railways it suddenly became possible to move large quantities of heavy materials from one place to another. Midlands brick and Welsh slate began to appear all over the country and house designs became increasingly standardised.

Shops and services

There has been a major change in shopping habits in the last ten or fifteen years. The number of small shops has more than halved. Supermarkets such as Sainsbury and Tesco have acquired an increasing share of the market. In 1980, for example, there were less than 250 superstores in the UK. Now there are nearly 1,000. This has had a major impact on many traditional town centres. It has also meant that people have become more and more dependent on using their cars for shopping.

Jobs

Employment is another area which is changing dramatically. Old industrial centres based on coal, ship-building, textiles and iron and steel have given way to warehousing, electronics and the service sector. It is often no longer possible to identify centres of production. Cars, for example, are assembled from components made in a number of different countries. At the same time structural unemployment has become a fact of life and many people have moved into new forms of work such as self-employment.

Journeys

Throughout history the speed of travel has depended largely on human effort and house power. In the past couple of hundred years, however, people have suddenly discovered new and faster ways of travelling. There are about 400 million cars in the world. Air travel is also becoming increasingly important for mass movement. These changes have had a major impact on the environment. Many people argue that we have reached the point where we have to alter our life styles in order to protect our surroundings.

Weather

The world is now warmer than at any time since the last Ice Age. Although it is impossible to predict long-term trends on short-term evidence, scientists believe that temperatures will continue to rise as 'global warming' begins to gather momentum. We can only speculate about the effects. Within a lifetime it is predicted that sea levels will rise by a metre or more due to expansion of the water. Weather patterns are also likely to be seriously disrupted.

Water

Water is arguably the most important of natural resources as it is fundamental to human life. In Western Europe we are accustomed to dependable supplies of clean piped water but there are growing fears of trace pollution from nitrate run-off and toxic chemicals. In the developing world the main problem is to obtain a safe water supply. Polluted water and inadequate sanitation are responsible for most diseases. The scandal is that simple technology and self help schemes could save millions of lives.

Materials and resources

We depend on natural resources for our modern way of life. Oil, for example, is essential for heating and transport as well as many manufactured products. Other minerals such as iron ore, tin and copper are also great sources of wealth. As consumption of raw materials has increased there are now fears that supplies will run out. People are becoming increasingly interested in recycling and conservation schemes. Alternative energy offers another way forward to a more sustainable future.

HOUSES ▶

Two localities should be studied. In these studies, pupils should be taught how land and buildings, *eg farms, parks, factories, houses,* are used.

Progression indicators
- describe the main parts of a house
- know that there are different types of houses
- explain why people need houses

Interpretation
The children should study houses and buildings in the local area and other places in the UK and overseas.

Introduction
Houses are a response to human needs. They provide protection from the weather and somewhere safe and secure for people to live. Although many modern houses are built to similar designs, there are still great differences around the world. In places where the weather is very hot and dry, for example, houses often have flat roofs as they do not have to cope with significant amounts of rain. The influence of the weather is most clearly seen in traditional designs where people use local materials in a variety of different ways.

Photographs and other secondary sources will provide information about houses in distant lands. However, children should also visit buildings in their own locality and study them at first hand if possible. As always when working with young children, it is best not to take anything for granted. In the reception class, for example, some children may not see houses as a whole building but, being small in stature, perceive them merely as walls and barriers.

Key vocabulary

address	garage
bedroom	home
chalet	kitchen
chimney	living room
detached	roof
door	terrace
flat	wall

Key questions
Why do people need houses?
Are all houses the same?
What are houses made from?
What other buildings are there in your area?

Resources

Poems
There are a number of poems about houses in *This Little Puffin*, compiled by Elizabeth Matterson (Puffin, 1969).

Rhymes

Here is a House

Here is a house built up high,
(Stretch arms up, touching fingertips)
With two tall chimneys reaching the sky.
(Stretch arms up separately)
Here are the windows
(Make square shape with hands)
Here is the door.
(Knock)
If we peep inside, we'll see a mouse on the floor.
(Raise hands in fright)

There was an Old Woman

There was an old woman
Who lived in a shoe.
She had so many children
She didn't know what to do.
She gave them some broth
Without any bread,
And whipped them all soundly,
And put them to bed.

Activity 141 Different buildings

Materials needed
Selection of magazines, scissors.

Make a list of all the different buildings the children can think of. Examples might include houses, shops, offices, garages, churches, cinemas, and so on. Use **Copymaster 72** (Different Buildings) to help the children link the names of buildings with their pictures. Give the children some old magazines and ask them to cut out any pictures of buildings they discover. Put these up as a wall display under the headings *This is where we live, This is where we work, This is where we spend our spare time.*

Activity 148 Name the parts

Materials needed
Large cardboard cut-out of a house, labels for the different parts.

Make a large cupboard cut-out of a house. This could open out so that the children first see the doors and windows and then look into the rooms. Get the children to name the different parts of the building. Can they match the labels to the correct room or part? What is each part of the house used for? Ask them to draw similar drawings of their own houses. They could include a picture of themselves in each of the rooms to help bring it to life. **Copymaster 73** (Houses) will reinforce the work and could provide an alternative way of teaching the same ideas if you do not have time to make a model.

Activity 149 Rooms with a purpose

Materials needed
Dolls' house, shoe boxes, pieces of wood, fabric and Plasticine.

Get the children to arrange the furniture and people in the dolls' house. See that there is a different activity going on in each room. Ask them to explain why they put the things in the places they have chosen. To extend the activity, get the children to make a model of a room using an old shoe box. Small pieces of wood and fabric are ideal for making furniture. Plasticine can be used for smaller items and for modelling figures. When the children have completed the work, ask them to draw a simple plan or picture showing the arrangement they

Name the parts. Get the children to pin labels to a model of a house.

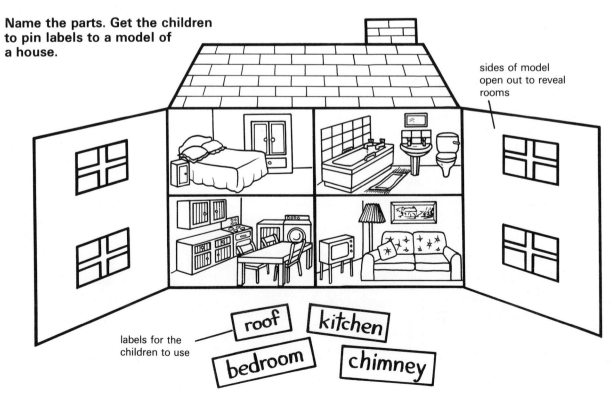

sides of model open out to reveal rooms

labels for the children to use

roof kitchen bedroom chimney

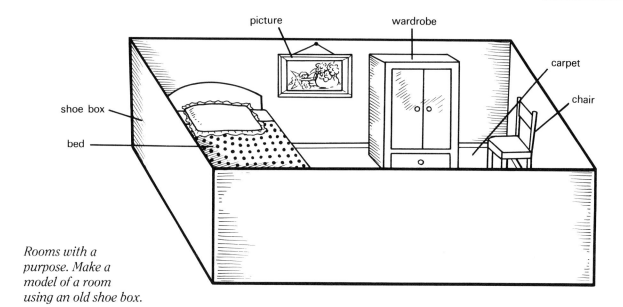

Rooms with a purpose. Make a model of a room using an old shoe box.

have created. This is a useful opportunity to introduce mapwork in context, and the children will already be very familiar with the layout of the objects.

Activity 150 Types of house

Materials needed
Pictures of houses, class scrap book.

Discuss with the children all the different types of homes that they know about. Examples will include houses that stand on their own, terraced houses, flats, bungalows, cottages, chalets, hotels, houseboats, cabins, summer houses, and so on. See if they can find an example of each one for a class scrap book. Write the name of the house underneath. Use **Copymaster 74** (House model) to extend the work.

Activity 151 Your address

Materials needed
Used postage stamps, glue.

Talk with the children about the different parts of an address. Explain that, in the UK, the name always comes first, followed by the house number, street, town, county and postcode. Get the children to write down their own address using **Copymaster 75** (My Address). Complete the exercise by cutting out the 'envelopes' and

glueing a used postage stamp in the top right-hand corner.

Activity 152 Animal addresses

Make up addresses for a number of different animals. You could prompt the children by talking about the habitats that creatures require. You will also find that animal stories provide a stimulus. For example, Bilbo Baggins' address is given in the opening pages of *The Hobbit*. Once they have got the idea, the children should be encouraged to make up addresses of their own.

Activity 153 House numbers

Talk about how people identify specific houses. In some places houses are given names, but numbers are much more common. Ask the children the number of their own house. Are the houses in their street numbered sequentially, or are they divided into odd and even? Working as a class, get the children to call out their house numbers. Record these on **Copymaster 76** (Odd and Even).

Activity 154 Front doors

Materials needed
Clipboards, paper and pencils.

Arrange a visit to a street near your school where the children can see the front doors of the houses from the

Animal addresses. Get the children to invent addresses for different animals.

pavement. Ask them to make careful drawings, paying special attention to the number, door handle and letter box. Mount the drawings as a display when you return to school. Alternatively, you could give the children **Copymaster 77** (My Front Door) to complete at home with the help of their parents.

Activity 155 Streets and houses

Materials needed

Crayons, small sheets of paper, a map of your locality.

Ask the children to make a drawing of their home using a pencil and crayons. Remind them to show the key features, such as the doors, windows, roof and chimney. Mount the pictures in the form of a map and add the names of local streets. See if the children can bring photographs of their homes to school to mount alongside their drawings. Collect further information using **Copymaster 78** (My Home).

Activity 156 Concertina book

Materials needed

Pictures and photographs of houses in different countries, card and Sellotape.

Make a collection of pictures of different homes and settlements around the world. You could provide some to start the project off, but the children should be encouraged to bring in their own examples from brochures, newspapers and colour supplements. Mount the pictures on pieces of card and fix them together to make a concertina book. The children will be excited by how the book grows, and the interest it provokes will provide a continual point of discussion. Talk about the age, location and materials used in the different buildings. Include some aerial photographs and a range of settlements from isolated farms to great cities. This is a project which could well extend over a considerable period. **Copymaster 79** (Houses Worldwide) could be introduced during this activity.

Activity 157 House shapes

Materials needed

Strips of coloured card, sugar paper, plastic Meccano/ construction kit, pictures of houses worldwide.

Consider different homes around the world. Show the children pictures or slides of a number of different examples. Draw their attention to the shape. Some houses have pitched roofs, others have flat roofs. Some are basically horizontal, others are vertical. Ask the children to make collage pictures using **Copymaster 80** (House Shapes), or get them to create models working with plastic Meccano or another construction kit. What shape are the houses in your own area?

Activity 158 Fantasy houses

Materials needed

Crayons, paints and other artwork materials.

Read the children the rhyme about the old woman who lived in the shoe (see page 62). Discuss how she fitted all

Homes Around the World

her family into such a small space. Where were the windows, chimney, front door and garden? Get the children to do paintings to show the old woman's house. Extend the idea by thinking about other unusual houses. How could a flower pot, Wellington boot or kettle be turned into a home? Who might live there, and why?

Blueprints links
The *Infant Geography Resource Bank* has a variety of copymasters which will help children learn about homes including sheet 10 'Types of homes' and sheet 68 'A new house'.

SHOPS AND SERVICES ▶

Pupils should be taught about the main physical and human features *eg rivers, hills, factories, shops,* that give the localities their character.

Progression indicators
- name different types of shops
- distinguish between goods and services
- understand the process of buying and selling

Interpretation
The children should know that there is a variety of shops selling different goods and that some people provide services which we use.

Introduction
Modern living depends on an extensive network of distribution systems. Water, electricity, gas and other utilities are brought directly to our homes. Food and other goods are delivered according to demand to hundreds of thousands of shops around the country. Young children need to know not only that farms produce food, but also the process by which it reaches us.

Infants enjoy playing in a shop corner, buying and selling things to each other. You could use this as a way of introducing the idea of goods. Role play also has great potential when it comes to considering services.

Ideally you should try to involve the children in fieldwork of one kind or another. Most schools are within walking distance of a high street or shopping parade. If the children can conduct their own enquiries and investigations, this will help to enhance the work.

Key vocabulary
General terms

deliver	market
electricity	post office
emergency	service
food	shop
gas	surgery
goods	telephone

Types of shop

baker	hardware
butcher	health food
chemist	jeweller
green grocer	newsagent

Key questions
Why do we need shops?
What are the different types of shop called?
How do shops obtain the things they sell?
What is the difference between goods and services?

Resources

Picture books
Shopping is a theme that features in quite a number of picture books. *The Shopping Basket* by John Burningham (Cape, 1980) is a humorous tale that involves a whole variety of different animals. *Wilberforce Goes Shopping* by Margaret Gordon (Kestrel, 1983) is one of a series of stories about Wilberforce the bear. Doreen Roberts adopts a more factual approach in *Joe's Day at the Market* (Oxford, 1973).

Song
'My Ship Sailed from China' from *Apusskidu* by Beatrice Harrop (Black, 1975).

Activity 159 Goods

Materials needed
Cardboard box, hat, glove, shoe, book, battery, food packets, stone, twig, feather, seashell.

Fill an empty cardboard box with a variety of items. Get the children to sort them into groups. They will probably find various ways of doing this, but after a while you could suggest that they sort them into things which are goods and things which are not. This should then lead to a discussion about where goods come from. **Copymaster 81** (Goods) will help to consolidate the children's ideas.

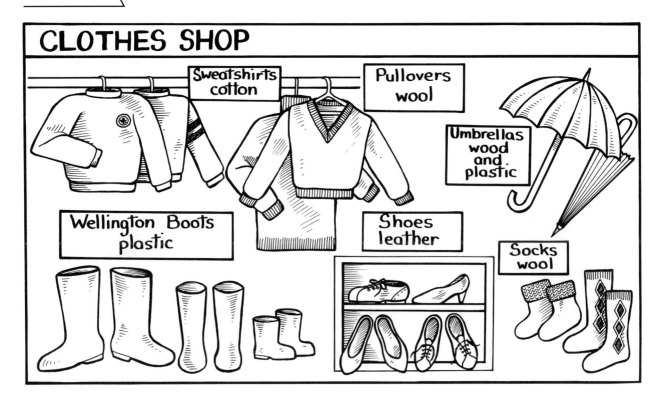

CLOTHES SHOP

(Labels: Sweatshirts cotton, Pullovers wool, Umbrellas wood and plastic, Wellington Boots plastic, Shoes leather, Socks wool)

Activity 160 Clothes shop

Materials needed

Photographs of clothing from magazines.

Ask the children to cut out photographs of clothing from magazines. Arrange the pictures as a collage on a display board. See if you can make it look like a clothes shop. Add labels for each item of clothing saying what it is and the material which it is made from.

Activity 161 Post office

Materials needed

Pens, pencils, forms, envelopes, used stamps, play money.

Set up a post office in a corner of the classroom. It will need a counter, and table tops for the customers to write on. Equip the post office with pens, pencils, forms, envelopes, stamps and play money. Allow the children to play at being customers and counter clerks. They might also make up letters and parcels for posting.

Activity 162 Advertisements

Materials needed

Advertisements for different services, class book.

Make a collection of advertisements for different services. You could start this off yourself and get the children to add to the collection using newspapers, brochures and the *Yellow Pages*. Put the advertisements into a class directory. Ask the children to add an advertisement of their own for a service that they can provide. In any class there are a surprising number of children who are 'expert' in one thing or another. Those who are not can always make something up.

Activity 163 Services in school

Materials needed

A large plan of the school.

Investigate services in your school. You could begin by considering the classroom. How are light, heat and water provided? Who organises repairs, cleaning and waste removal? Is any food prepared in the school? What happens if a child is hurt in the playground? How are messages received and sent? Fix a large plan of the school on to the wall of the classroom. Get the children to add labels for telephones, dustbins, first aid, kitchens, and so on. Extend the idea using **Copymaster 82** (Services).

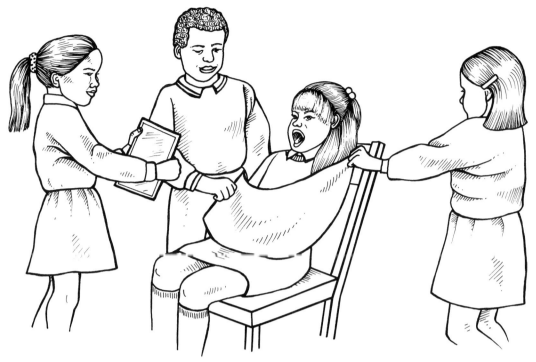

Roleplay. Ask the children to act out a scene.

Activity 164 Role play

Talk with the children about the different people who provide a service, such as doctors, dentists, teachers and police officers. Divide the class into small groups and get them to act out a short scene involving someone who provides a service. Ask them to perform it to the rest of the class. Can the other children work out what is going on? What service is being provided?

Activity 165 Shopping street

Materials needed

Large cardboard boxes, magazines, modelling and artwork materials.

Obtain some large cardboard boxes and cut these in half down the middle. Working in small groups or individually, the children can then use the boxes to make some model shops. They will need to decide what their shop sells. Is it a chemist, newsagent or grocer's? Get the children to give their shop a name, and see if they can find any pictures of goods in magazines to cut out and put on the 'shelves'. When they are finished you could arrange the models along one of the walls of the classroom to make a shopping street. If the children put flaps across the shop windows you might get other children to guess what each shop sells.

The newsagent

The grocer's

The chemist

Shopping street. Make models of shops from cardboard boxes.

Activity 166 Adopt a shop

Either working as a class or in groups, 'adopt' one of the shops in the neighbourhood. Ask the shopkeeper to come and talk about what he or she does. When does the shop open and close? Who works there? When do they go on holiday? Where do the goods come from? How long has the shop been there? See if the shopkeeper can explain about ordering stock. How do the people running the shop decide what to order? How is it done, and who delivers the goods?

Activity 167 Markets

Materials needed

Plasticine, photographs of markets around the world.

Make a plasticine model of a market stall. It might be selling food, clothes, household goods or electrical equipment. Put different models together to make a complete scene. The children might then add livestock. They could record the layout on a plan. Talk to the children about markets they have visited. Why do people still like to use them when big stores sell goods in more comfortable surroundings? Widen the discussion by looking at photographs of markets around the world. What can you learn from the pictures? What are the similarities and differences with markets in the United Kingdom?

Activity 168 Networks

Materials needed

Large pieces of paper, crayons.

Organise a short walk round the streets near your school. Get the children to look for all the different goods and services clues they can find. These might include telephone boxes, fire hydrants, manhole covers in the pavement, shop signs, and so on. Use **Copymaster 83** (Different Clues) as a way of recording information. What can the children learn from the things they have discovered? Can they describe other parts of the

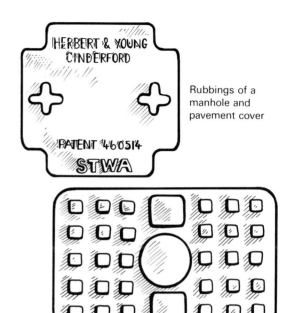

Rubbings of a manhole and pavement cover

network and see how they link together? Make rubbings of a variety of manhole and other pavement covers. Put them up as a class display and arrange them in groups – water, gas, electricity and telephone.

Activity 169 Links

Materials needed

Puzzle box containing a piece of wool, a milk bottle top, something made of wood, and other items.

Discuss with the children what the items in the box all have in common. The conclusion should be that they all come from the countryside. Discuss the jobs that might be involved in producing each material and distributing it. For example, the milk bottle top is part of a chain which involves the farmer, milk lorry driver, dairy worker, bottle maker, manager, milkman and cashier/accountant. The children could record some of these sequences by setting up a flow chart as a class display.

Blueprints links

The *Infant Geography Resource Bank* has a sequence of copymasters (41–68) tracing how different things are made or produced and supplied to the shops. Studies include milk, strawberries, fish fingers, coal, bricks, woollen clothes and timber products.

JOBS ▶

Two localities should be studied. In these studies, pupils should be taught how land and buildings, *eg farms, parks, factories, houses*, are used.

Progression indicators
- talk about the difference between work and play
- know about different jobs done in school
- compare different types of job

Interpretation

The children should find about jobs and work in their school and immediate vicinity and in other places in the UK or overseas.

Introduction

There are many different types of work. Some people stay indoors, others work outside. Jobs can require physical strength or mental activity. Sometimes people work on their own, more frequently they form part of a team.

Most infants have very little idea of what people do when they go to work. The impression that they gain by watching adults at school (most of whom exercise a form of parental care) is rather misleading.

Young children will need assistance in drawing conclusions from what they observe. For example, the postman does not merely walk from house to house; he delivers letters. It is important to move beyond what is immediately obvious. You might also take the opportunity to challenge sex stereotypes. For example, are there any jobs which are only done by men or women?

If possible, arrange for adults to visit the class bringing any special equipment or materials which they use in their work. You might also be able to arrange a visit to a farm or some other work place. Photographs provide another valuable resource. The links with art, music, English and drama could all be developed to extend the project.

Key vocabulary

assistant	helper	shift
caretaker	holiday	shopkeeper
cook	job	skill
dentist	nurse	teacher
doctor	office	work
factory	postman	
farm	secretary	

Key questions

What is work?
What jobs do people do locally?
Can they be divided into categories?
Who organises them?

Resources

Picture books

The Postman Pat stories by John Cunliffe (published by André Deutsch and Hippo Books) have proved very popular with young children over the years, and help to introduce the idea of work. Postal services also feature in *Katie Morag Delivers the Mail* by Mairi Hedderwick (Bodley, 1984). It is worth noting that all the Katie Morag books are set on the Isle of Struay and have a picture map on the inside front cover.

Poems

The Policeman

The policeman walks with a heavy tread,
Left, right, left, right,
Swings his arms, holds up his head,
Left, right, left, right.

(Children mime as the words suggest.)

Soldiers

See the soldiers in the street,
Hear the marching of their feet;
They are singing as they go,
Marching, marching, to and fro.
See the soldiers in the street,
Hear the marching of their feet.

(Children march round separately in a long line to the tune of 'Twinkle, twinkle, little star'.)

Songs

Suitable songs include 'On a Work Day I Work' from *Every Colour Under the Sun* by Redvers Brandling (Black, 1983) and 'The Fireman' from *Apusskidu* by Beatrice Harrop (Black, 1975).

Activity 170 What is work?

Split the class into groups and give the children a range of activities and exercises to do. These might include number work, reading, modelling, painting, and so on. Get the children to change activities every 15 minutes so that they do a mixture of different things. At the end of the session get the children to discuss what they did. Which things were fun, which things were hard work? Were any activities particularly popular? Does work need to be unpleasant? How do we know when we are working?

Activity 171 School jobs

Talk with the children about the different people who work in your school. Discuss what jobs they do. Make lists of (a) people who work in school every day and (b) people who visit the school. **Copymaster 84** (School Jobs) is designed to prompt ideas. You should check that the children can read the words and understand what they mean before they begin.

Activity 172 Job fact files

Materials needed
Rectangles of light card in different colours.

Make a display of fact files about the different jobs done in your school. Each fact file should give the name of the person, the job that they do, the hours that they work and the part of the building that they use. The children should collect this information by conducting simple interviews. They could also make drawings of each person to go with the fact files in the display. **Copymaster 85** (Counting the Jobs) provides a supporting activity.

Activity 173 Music while you work

Sing some of the songs which people have invented to make their job easier and to pass the time in repetitive and physically-demanding work. Examples include 'Heigh Ho, It's off to work we go!' and sea shanties. Develop some of these ideas in movement lessons by getting some of the children to act out the different jobs

CARETAKER

Name : Mr James

Job : Looks after the school building

Begins work : 7·00

Finishes work : 6·00

Place of work : All round the school

– lifting the anchor, digging a trench, and so on. Can other children guess what it is they are doing?

Activity 174 Running a school

Materials needed
Sugar paper, felt tips.

Make a list of the things which are needed to keep a school going. This might include electricity, gas, water, telephones, books, food, repairs and emergency services. Put the list up on the wall as a display. Ask the children to decide who provides these different things. Make a list of jobs in a separate column.

Activity 175 People who help us
Discuss the different people who help the children in some way as part of their job. Examples might include nurses, doctors, the police, Post Office workers, shop assistants, and so on. Get the children to make paintings of these different people for a class display. They can make each person look different by showing the uniform that they wear or something distinctive that they use. Extend the work using **Copymaster 86** (Parcel Post). Consider the different jobs which are

done at home. Are people always paid for the things they do? Can the children think of any volunteer or charity workers that they know of? Why do they not get paid?

Activity 176 Places of work

Materials needed
Photographs or pictures of people doing different indoor jobs.

Give the children photographs or pictures of people who work at different indoor jobs. These might include a nurse, a teacher, a librarian, a chef or a waitress. Ask the children to paint the place where each person works. Pin the pictures up as a class display and put labels under each one saying what it shows.

Activity 177 A dictionary of jobs

Materials needed
Pictures from magazines.

Working with the children, make a list of as many different jobs as possible. Can you find a job for every

PEOPLE WHO HELP US

milkman   nurse   policewoman caretaker   doctor

A Dictionary of Jobs

A is for acrobat. Acrobats work at the circus.

B is for builder. Builders make houses.

letter in the alphabet? Make up a dictionary of jobs as a wall display. Get the children to write a sentence describing each one. Cut out a picture to illustrate each job from old magazines. If it proves impossible to find all the pictures you need, the children could do drawings instead.

Activity 178 Jobs around the world

Materials needed
Photographs and pictures of people around the world.

Collect and display photographs of people doing work in other parts of the world. These might include 'formal' work for an employer, 'informal' work in which people earn a living for themselves (for example, by cleaning shoes) and unpaid work (collecting water and firewood).

The various aid agencies are a good source of teaching materials (see address list, page 90). Discuss why people do these different jobs. Is there any evidence that men and women do different work? How are jobs changing?

Activity 179 Street work

Materials needed
Light card, Sellotape, glue.

Ask the children to look carefully at the things they see on their way to and from school. How many people do they see who are doing a job? What work are they doing? Are they always working in the same place, or do they move around? Make a concertina book for the children to display their notes and drawings in. You can add to this over a period of time as the children notice more and more things. You could also make a simple quiz to go with it. The questions might ask 'Who uses a ladder?' 'Who uses a hard hat?' Who works from a van?', and so on.

Activity 180 Tools and equipment

Materials needed
Paintbrush, spanner, piece of chalk, calculator, cleaning cloth.

Set up a small display of equipment that different people use as part of their job. Let the children examine the different items and talk about what they think they are. Who might use them and why? How do tools and equipment help us in our work? Which jobs require lots of equipment? Which ones require hardly any? Ask the children to complete **Copymaster 87** (Equipment) to extend and consolidate the work.

Activity 181 Acting a job

Materials needed
Dressing-up clothes, a collection of workers' hats.

Turn the play corner into a shop, factory or some other place of work. Allow the children to choose the workplace and organise themselves. Then discuss the job each one is going to do. Have they remembered all the different workers? In a shop, for example, there might be a counter assistant, manager shelf-filler, cleaner, delivery driver and health inspector. Encourage

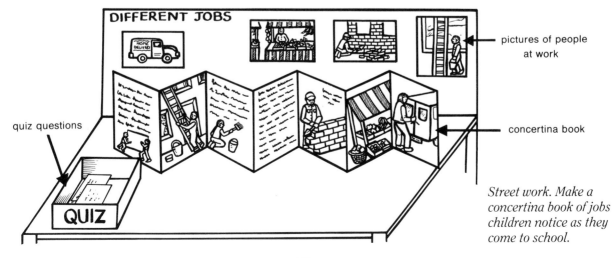

Street work. Make a concertina book of jobs children notice as they come to school.

the children to take on a variety of different roles. One way of doing this is to provide them with a number of different hats. These are fairly easy to improvise and can be cut out of card. **Copymaster 88** (Different Hats) might help to stimulate ideas. Get the children to act out the different roles. Can other children guess what they are? Which role do they prefer, and why?

Activity 182 Car production line

Materials needed
Crayons or felt tips, scissors, glue, frieze paper.

Set up a simple car production line. You will need to divide the children into groups and get each group to produce a different part – the wheels, body or windows. **Copymaster 89** (Production Line) provides cut-outs

for the children to use. See how many pieces the children can colour in a given time. Give other children the task of glueing the parts together. How many complete cars can be assembled? Mount them on frieze paper. What are the advantages of having a production line? Can the children think of any disadvantages?

Activity 183 A place of work
Arrange a visit to a place of work in your locality. A shop, supermarket or office might prove suitable. List the different jobs that people do. Get the children to make a sample study of just one occupation. They might ask a few simple questions using **Copymaster 90** (Job Questionnaire). What jobs would the children like to do when they are grown up? Get them to give reasons for their answers.

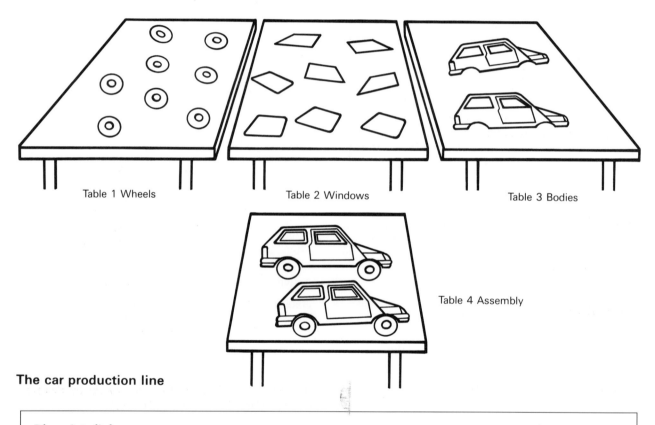

Table 1 Wheels   Table 2 Windows   Table 3 Bodies

Table 4 Assembly

The car production line

Blueprints links
There is a section on 'People Who Help Us' in the *Infant Geography Resource Bank*. Relevant copymasters include sheet 69 'At the hospital', sheet 71 'At the fire station' and sheet 73 'The police'. Many of the other copymasters, eg sheet 50 'The strawberry story' show people at work and are ideal both for discussion and as a source of reference.

JOURNEYS

Pupils should be given opportunities to undertake studies that are based on direct experience, practical activities and fieldwork in the locality of the school.

Progression indicators
- name different types of transport
- know how people find their way on a journey
- compare different routes

Interpretation

The children should describe the journeys they make to school by car, bus, bicycle, taxi, and on foot. They should also discuss and record how people make journeys of different lengths when they go shopping, see friends or travel to work.

Introduction

The journeys which people make and the way that they travel have always been of interest to geographers. In the past, most people travelled on foot or by animal. Nowadays, cars, buses, trains, boats and aeroplanes link many places together. Each major transport system has its own routes. The way that these inter-relate tells a complex and fascinating story.

This unit introduces children to the idea of communications. It also involves the study of routes and raises questions about the means of transport. Many young children travel from place to place in the back of a car and sometimes gain little impression of the places that they visit. As a result they may have little direct experience of journeys which the teacher can develop.

There are good opportunities for studying routes in the classroom and school building. This is a good place to begin, as it is an environment which is familiar to the children. When they become more confident you can consider the local area, using examples such as the journey to school. Holidays in distant locations and other countries introduces another dimension. You could also develop the work through picture books and stories. Even if the children have not travelled far in reality, it is always possible to visit places overseas in their imaginations.

Key vocabulary

General terms

abroad	journey
delivery	obstacle
direction	route
holiday	travel

Types of vehicle

aeroplane	car
bicycle	ferry
boat	taxi
bus	train

Transport facilities

airport	railway
motorway	road
port	station

Key questions

Why do people go on journeys?
What vehicles do they use?
What are the advantages and disadvantages of walking?
How do people know which way to go?
What obstacles get in the way?

Resources

Picture books

Children's stories often describe journeys. Examples include *Mr Gumpy's Motor Car* by John Burningham (Cape, 1973) and *The Riverboat Crew* by Andrew McLean (Oxford, 1978). Some journeys, such as the one in *Rosie's Walk* by Pat Hutchins (Bodley, 1968) also suggest a definite route which children can map.

Poems

Read the children 'The Owl and the Pussycat' by Edward Lear. How did the owl and the pussycat travel? What preparations did they make, and what happened to them?

Rhymes

One Big Tanker Goes Rolling By

One big tanker goes rolling by.
How many big wheels can you spy?
Two big tankers go rolling by.
How many big wheels can you spy?
Three big tankers go rolling by.
How many big wheels can you spy?
Four big tankers go rolling by.
How many big wheels can you spy?
Five big tankers go rolling by.
How many big wheels can you spy?

Songs

'The Train is A-Coming' from *Apusskidu* by Beatrice Harrop (Black, 1975) is a popular song.

Activity 184 Journeys around the school

Materials needed

Pins, wool, plan of the school.

Get the children to talk about different journeys they make from the classroom to other parts of the school. They might go to the toilets, other classrooms, the secretary's office, library area, playground, and so on. Using pins and wool, plot these journeys on a large, clear plan of your school. Which are the shortest and longest journeys? Which journeys only involve going through one door? Which journeys involve going through two or three doors? See if the children can make up puzzle journeys which they can describe to each other (the other children have to guess where the journey ends). Use **Copymaster 91** (Different Journeys) as a way of developing the work.

Activity 185 Reasons for travel

Materials needed
Large, clear plan of the school.

Discuss in detail some of the journeys which the children identified in the previous activity. Use the map as a way of prompting further ideas. What would the children find at the places they have selected? How many different reasons can they think of for going there? What other parts of the school can children visit on their own? What parts do they go to occasionally, and why? Where do they never go?

Activity 186 Journey survey

Materials needed
Ordnance Survey map of the local area.

Get the children to keep a record of all the journeys they make over a number of days. **Copymaster 92** (Journey Survey) is an empty survey sheet which the children can complete. You should make it clear that they only need to record journeys to specific places. There is no need for them to record every time they go out to play. However, if they go for a walk to the park then that would count. When the survey is complete you should discuss the results. Can the children find the different places on an Ordnance Survey map of the area? What form of transport was used most? What was the main reason for journeys?

Activity 187 Ways of travelling

Materials needed
Small pieces of card, glue, scissors.

Make a survey of how children in your class come to school. You could either get the children to draw symbols of their method of transport on a piece of card, or cut them out from **Copymaster 93** (Ways of Travelling). Arrange the symbols to create a pictogram. What form of transport is used most? Is there any reason for this? Get the children to consider the route that they take. What are the obstacles that get in their way? Would it be quicker for them to come by any other means?

Activity 188 Near or far?

Materials needed
Drawing paper, crayons/felt tips, coloured wool, drawing pins, large-scale Ordnance Survey map of the school locality.

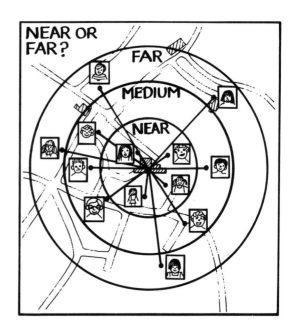

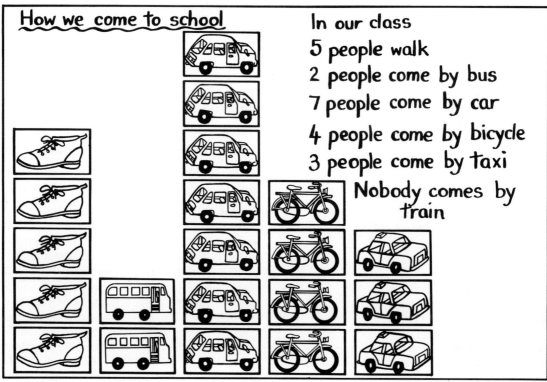

Getting to school survey

Draw a simplified version of the Ordnance Survey map of your school locality and fix it to the wall where all the children can see it. Get each child to identify where they live and mark their home with a drawing pin. The children should then draw pictures of themselves on small pieces of drawing paper. Place each picture next to the correct pin and connect it to the school using wool or string. Finally, overlay three concentric rings to show distance bands – near, medium and far. Discuss the display with the children. Who has the longest and shortest journeys? How long do they take?

Activity 189 Journey to school

Find out more about the children's journey to school. **Copymaster 94** (Journey to School) provides a series of structured questions which the children could complete for themselves and take home for parents to check. You could then discuss and compare the results. Do children who live near the school always have the shortest journeys? Which is the longest journey made on foot, and by car? What are the main obstacles and dangers?

Activity 190 Transport survey

Go into the playground and make a survey of all the different vehicles that you see in a five-minute period. You might see cars, vans, lorries, bicycles, motorbikes and buses on the road, trains on nearby railway lines and aeroplanes in the sky. **Copymaster 95** (Transport Survey) will help you record the results. Which vehicles appear to be used most? Which vehicles are used least? It is interesting to repeat the survey at a different time of day to see if there are changes. You could also ask the children to think about vehicles which they know about but did not see. Examples might include ships, helicopters and underground trains.

Activity 191 Vehicle collage

Materials needed
Old magazines, scissors, glue.

Give the children some old magazines and ask them to cut out any pictures of vehicles that they discover. Put the pictures up on the wall as a collage. Get the children to add labels naming each vehicle and saying what it carries. Try to include a range of examples. For instance, if the children can find a picture of a cement

mixer, a Post Office van or a horse box it will help to promote discussion. As an alternative, they might make their own drawings of some more unusual vehicles from books. **Copymaster 96** (Car Game) is one way of extending the work in a light-hearted manner.

Activity 192 Bus journeys

Which of the children in the class have been on a bus? Discuss their journeys and list the places they went to. Use **Copymaster 97** (Bus Journeys) to make a class picture. You could put all the buses together to make a bus depot, or you could spread them out along a road. Ask the children to bring in bus timetables and old bus tickets. Are any of the children's parents or relatives bus drivers or conductors? See if you can arrange for them to come and speak to the class about their work, the people they meet and the places they go to.

Activity 193 Deliveries

Materials needed
Yellow Pages directory, map of the local area, card and other modelling equipment.

Look in the local *Yellow Pages* to find the nearest suppliers for coal, fish, cement and stone. Make up a wall map with copies or cut-outs of the different advertisements. Use the map to work out the route that different delivery vehicles would take to your school. Get the children to make a vehicle to deliver a bag of coal or a block of stone, using card and other modelling materials.

Activity 194 Places to visit

Talk about different sections of the community, such as old age pensioners, teenagers and mothers with young children. What journeys are they likely to make and for what purpose? What type of transport could they use? Are there any problems which make it hard for them to travel when and where they want to? Explore this idea further using **Copymaster 98** (Places to Visit).

Activity 195 Direction signs

Materials needed
Card, felt tips.

Make a study of a direction sign in your locality. Visit it with the children and discuss what it shows. Get them

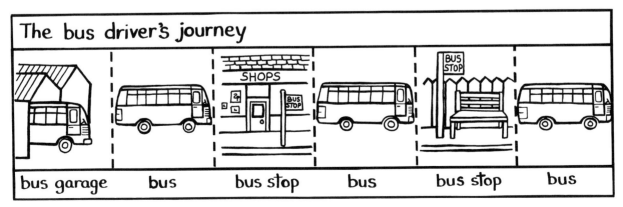

Bus journeys. Make a frieze showing where people go in their daily work.

to make careful sketches so that they can make a card model of it when they return to school. Look at maps of your area to find the places named on the sign. Have any of the children been there? Was it a long journey? What other direction signs do they know of?

Activity 196 Obstacles

Discuss the different obstacles people have to overcome when they make journeys. Bridges, viaducts and embankments help us to cross valleys. Cuttings and tunnels pierce mountains. Ferries and air services link places separated by the sea. Get the children to make drawings of some of these things or ask them to colour and complete **Copymaster 99** (Obstacles) by joining the dots.

Activity 197 Toy vehicles

Materials needed

Toy vehicles, cardboard tubes, paper straws, cotton reels, small pieces of wood and other modelling equipment.

Set up a display of different toy vehicles and discuss how they are used. Get the children to arrange them on a display board as a traffic jam at a road junction. Ask them to bring some of their own toys from home to add to the collection. Can the children sort them into different groups, for example vehicles which carry people, vehicles which carry goods? Set them a challenge to design a vehicle that will carry a toy brick. You could provide a range of modelling equipment such

as cardboard tubes, cotton reels, paper straws and small pieces of wood. Ask the children to talk about the problems they had to solve in making their model.

Activity 198 Holiday journeys

Materials needed

Paper, string or wool, card, artwork materials.

Ask the children where they have been during the holidays and how they travelled there. This might involve a simple questionnaire which the children take home to complete with their parents. **Copymaster 100** (Holiday Journeys) is designed for this purpose. As some of the children will not go away for a holiday, emphasise that they might have made a short trip, such as to the park. Make a display of the information you have collected. Start by asking the children to draw a picture of themselves, and get them to write a sentence underneath saying where they went and how they travelled. You should then ask them to fix their drawing on to a display board. You can convey the idea of distance using three concentric rings. The first or inner ring will show destinations near to home, the middle ring destinations elsewhere in the United Kingdom, and the outer ring destinations abroad. Add lines of string or wool connecting each picture to the centre of the display and discuss any patterns that emerge. For example, did most of the children who visited places near to home travel by car? Did those who went abroad travel by plane?

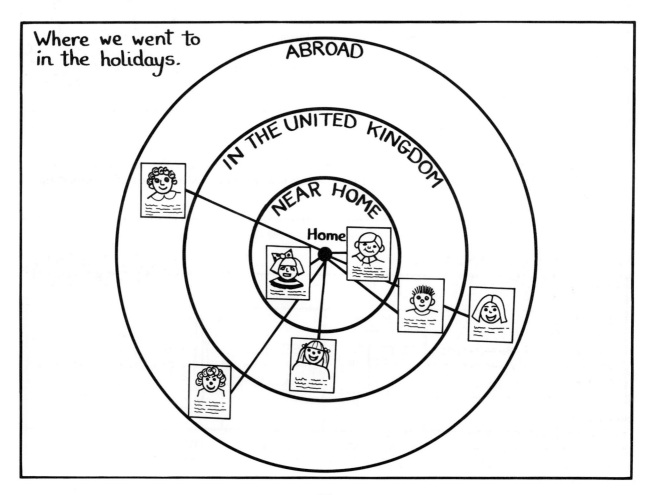

Activity 199 Adventure journeys

Materials needed
Travel stories, slides and videos, world map or globe.

Read the children some true accounts of journeys of exploration and adventure. These could include safaris, mountain expeditions, long-distance sailing races or space travel. Discuss and map the journeys. Try to find out details of how the people travelled, the dangers that they faced and the things they saw. Why did they go on the journey? Use this information as a stimulus to encourage the children to write some adventure stories of their own. Get them to include some real place names and features from a world map.

Activity 200 Stories of journeys
Get the children to talk about stories and poems that they know of which involve a journey. *Rosie's Walk* is a good example. Ask the children to make a map showing the different places that Rosie visits. Make sure that they add the names of some of the key features. Check carefully that the features are in the correct order. Could another child follow the map they have drawn?

Round the World Yacht Race

Blueprints links
Many of the copymasters in the *Infant Geography Resource Bank* consider journeys in one way or another. Sheets 77–80 are especially relevant as they consist of drawings of a motorway, underground station, airport and railway.

WEATHER

Two localities should be studied. In these studies, pupils should be taught about the effects of weather on people and their surroundings, *eg the effect of seasonal variations in temperature on the clothes people wear*.

Progression indicators
- name different types of weather
- describe seasonal weather patterns
- suggest how people are affected by the weather

Interpretation
The children should observe and record the weather in their own environment. They should also be taught about different seasons and weather conditions in this country and abroad.

Introduction

The weather has a profound effect on our lives. It influences our moods, the clothes we wear, the houses we live in, and how we spend our spare time. Long-term weather patterns (climates) are even more crucial as they determine the crops that can be grown. It is salutary to remember that we still depend on farming and agriculture for our survival. This is one of the reasons why global warming presents such a serious threat.

In these days of central heating and door-to-door transport, children are often isolated from natural processes. One of the best ways of making them aware of the weather is through direct experience. You could get the children to make their own weather records and observations.

Another approach is to consider the seasons. Even the youngest children are aware of winter snowfall, summer holidays and the growth of plants in spring. School festivals like Christmas and Easter help to emphasise this pattern. You might develop the work by looking at weather conditions in other parts of the world. Extremes of hot and cold provide vivid images which capture the imagination and help to stimulate the children's interest.

Key vocabulary

autumn	gale	storm
breeze	hail	summer
calm	hot	symbol
cloud	ice	thunder
cold	mild	warm
drizzle	rain	weather
dry	season	wet
dull	shower	windy
fog	snow	winter
frost	spring	

Key questions

How can we record the weather?
Is there a pattern to the weather?
What clues tell us about the seasons?
Why does the weather change?
What is the weather like in other places?

Resources

Legends

The weather and seasons often feature in traditional tales and legends. The story of Demeter and Persephone can be found in many anthologies of Greek myths. You might also explore links with other cultures in countries such as India and China, and the Caribbean.

Picture books

The Weather Cat by Helen Cresswell (Collins, 1989) is a gentle story about a cat that can forecast the weather.

Cloudy with a Chance of Meat Balls by Judi Barrett (Gollancz, 1980) is a rather more dramatic tale about a land where it rains food. All goes well until the weather takes a turn for the worse.

Poems and rhymes

There is a range of weather poems in *The Possum Tree* by Lesley Pyott (Black, 1985), as well as in many other anthologies. 'Incey Wincey Spider' is a popular rhyme.

Incey Wincey Spider

Incey wincey spider,
Climbing up the spout;
Down came the rain,
And washed the spider out;
Out came the sun,
And dried up all the rain;
Incey wincey spider,
Climbing up again.

Songs

There is a wide choice of weather songs. One that often proves popular is 'The North Wind Doth Blow' from *The Music Box Songbook* compiled by Barry Gibson (BBC, 1987).

Activity 201 Weather words

Materials needed

Photographs from magazines and newspapers, light card.

Make a collection of photographs and pictures from newspapers and magazines showing different types of weather. Talk with the children about what the pictures show. What words would they use to describe the weather conditions? Get the children to write labels to pin under each picture. When they have completed the work, play a game by taking the labels away and asking the children to put them back where they belong.

Activity 202 Weather symbols

Materials needed

Small pieces of card, crayons, felt tips and flash cards.

Make a set of flash cards based on weather words such as rain, wind, cloud, sun, snow. Give the children some small pieces of card and ask them to draw symbols to go with each word. Alternatively, you could give them **Copymaster 101** (Weather Snap) to colour and cut out. Use the symbols and flash cards in some simple matching games. Snap and Pelmanism both provide useful models.

Activity 203 Experiencing the weather

Materials needed
Sugar paper, scissors, felt tips.

Take the children into the playground and talk with them about the weather. How does it make them feel? Could they describe it to someone far away? When you return to the classroom, get the children to make a large cut out figure of a person for a wall display. You could ask a child to lie on the floor and get the others to draw round the outline on to sugar paper. Add labels describing the weather. Repeat the same exercise on a contrasting day later in the week and put up a second display using an outline figure and labels in the same way.

Activity 205 Recording the weather

Materials needed
A large sheet of card, paper, crayons, felt tips, scissors.

Get the children to make a set of words and symbols for different weather conditions. They should draw these on small squares of paper so that they pin them up on a weather chart. Ask the children to select the correct word and symbol for each different day. At the end of the week add up the totals. Has it been mostly cloudy, sunny, or rainy? You could continue to keep records for a period of a month and enter them into a computer database as part of a project in technology.

OUR WEATHER CHART		
DAY	WEATHER	WORD
Monday	☀	SUNNY
Tuesday	☀	SUNNY
Wednesday	🌧	RAINY

Activity 204 All in a day

Make two separate visits to the playground to record the weather, once in the morning and once in the afternoon. Does it feel warm or cold? Is it calm or windy? Ask the children to complete **Copymaster 102** (All in a Day). Was there any difference between the morning and afternoon? Discuss what might happen to the weather during the evening.

Activity 206 Weather dial

Materials needed
Light card, paper fasteners, felt tips and crayons, scissors.

Get the children to make weather dials from light card. The first step is to cut out a house shape with a window on the right-hand side. The children should then cut out a card circle and draw weather symbols around the edge. To assemble the dial they fix the circle behind the

Weather dial

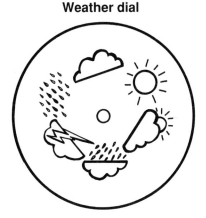

What is the weather like today?

WEATHER DIAL
What is the weather● like today?

Card house shape with cut-out window   Card circle with weather symbols   Completed dial with paper fastener

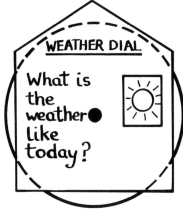

house with a paper fastener. As they turn the dial the different symbols will appear. They should set the weather window each day to record different conditions. Before you begin this activity you might find it helpful to make a dial of your own so that you can show the children what it looks like.

Activity 207 Weather forecast

Materials needed
Doll/teddy bear with clothes, question and answer cards.

Bring a doll or teddy bear to school to act as a weather 'forecaster'. Decide on the weather each morning and dress the bear in the correct set of clothes for the day. You could make a set of question and answer cards to include in the display. For example, the question might be 'What's the weather like today, teddy?'. The children then have to select the right answer, such as 'It's warm and sunny'. You might also talk about different ways of forecasting the weather and find out about traditional weather proverbs as part of the work.

Activity 208 The right weather

Talk with the children about how the weather affects our lives. Has the weather ever spoilt what they were doing? Can they think of different activities which can only be done if the weather is right? Swimming out of doors and tobogganing are cases in point. Get them to complete **Copymaster 103** (The Right Weather) as a way of developing this theme. You might also ask the children to make drawings of some of the activities for a class display.

Activity 209 Wind testers

Materials needed
Balloon, string, paper, scissors, gardening sticks, nails, card, Sellotape.

Make a number of different wind testers to use in the playground. These could include a balloon on a piece of string, a paper fish, a simple windmill and a streamer. Using the testers, find out if there is a strong breeze, light breeze, dead calm and so on. Which of the devices seems most sensitive? Are some parts of the playground windier than others?

Activity 210 Weather picture

Materials needed
General artwork materials including paints and brushes.

Divide a display board into four sections: wet, windy, sunny and cold. Ask the children to paint a picture or make a collage of the type of weather they like most. Pin their work up on the correct part of the display board, together with explanatory sentences such as 'I like windy weather because it's exciting' or 'When it rains I enjoy playing in puddles'.

Activity 211 Weather music

Materials needed
Musical instruments.

Compose some different pieces of music with the children to evoke different types of weather. For example, they might choose a lazy summer's day or a storm at sea as their theme. Can they capture this musically? What instruments and sounds are most appropriate? When the composition is complete, invite another class to come and listen to a performance. Can they guess the weather that the children had in mind?

Activity 212 Season tree

Materials needed
Cotton wool, tissue paper, paints and crayons, scissors, glue.

Make a picture of four large outline trees for a class display. Get the children to complete each one as a seasonal collage. Add blossom for the spring, green leaves for the summer, falling leaves in yellow and brown for the autumn and put snow on the branches for winter. Use **Copymaster 104** (Seasonal dial) to help the children match the seasons with the calendar months.

Activity 213 Seasonal words

Put the names of the seasons as headings on a display board. Get the children to write out all the weather words they can think of and pin them under the headings where they think they belong. Discuss the reasons for their choices. Add other words to do with

Wind testers

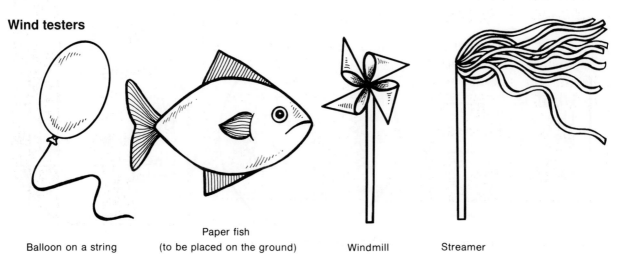

Balloon on a string   Paper fish (to be placed on the ground)   Windmill   Streamer

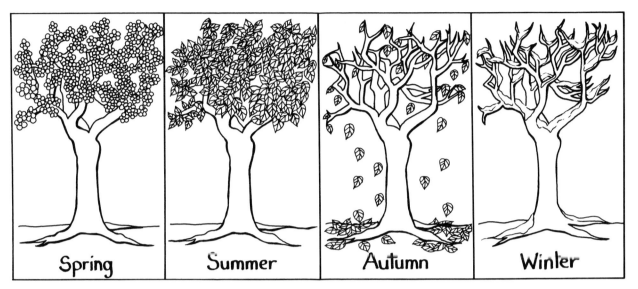

Season tree. Make a collage of seasonal changes.

seasonal activities. Think about the life cycles of plants and animals. How do the seasons affect what we do and the clothes we wear?

Activity 214 Poetry box

Materials needed
Light card, scissors, glue.

Working as a class, make a list of words to describe the current season. Use these as the starting point for a poetry lesson. There is no need to make the poems complicated. A few contrasting words and phrases can convey the character of a season with great effect. You could extend the work by asking the children to write a different poem for each season. They could then decorate the poems and glue them on to a strip of card to make an open box. This creates an attractive table decoration which the children can take home to show their parents.

Activity 215 Seasonal cluedo
Here is a list of clues for spring and autumn.

Spring	Autumn
Blossom	Storms
Tadpoles	Falling leaves
Lambs	Conkers
Daffodils	Bonfires
Cuckoos	Harvest
Sowing seeds	Berries
Birds' nests	Toadstools
Buds and leaves	Dew
Showers	

Write each of these clues on a piece of card. It would be helpful if you could add drawings or pictures to go with each one. Arrange the classroom with two large tables opposite each other and a large space for the children to sit in the middle. Put a label 'Spring Clues' on one of the tables and label the other one 'Autumn Clues'. You might put a child in charge of each table and give them a special spring or autumn hat.

Place the cards on the floor and get the children to read them out one at a time. The class should then discuss which table they think each card should be

Poetry box. Get the children to write short seasonal poems.

81

placed on. When the game has finished the children can record the words on **Copymaster 105** (Spring and Autumn Clues). To extend the game the children could decide on clues for winter and summer in the same way.

Activity 216 Dressed for the season

Materials needed
Dressing-up clothes, old cardboard boxes.

Divide the clothes in the dressing-up corner into seasonal collections. One way of doing this is to set up four large cardboard boxes, one for each season. Get the children to label the boxes and draw pictures on the front. They can then play at dressing up for different times of the year, while other members of the class guess which season they have chosen. Winter and summer are easy to distinguish but autumn and spring will be much less clear-cut. In our climate each season

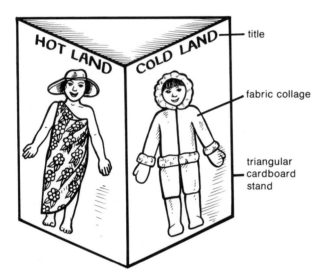

can have a wide variety of weather. Extend the work using **Copymaster 106** (The Right Clothes).

Activity 217 Clothes

Materials needed
Pieces of fabric of different textures and colours, scissors, glue, pictures of people in different costumes.

Discuss the different clothes that we wear. Why do we need a variety of clothes? How do we deal with very cold, hot or wet weather? Look at pictures of people in other parts of the world. What do their clothes tell us about the weather? **Copymasters 107** and **108** (Clothes 1 and 2) provide outlines which the children can 'dress' using pieces of fabric. When they have completed the sheets they should cut round the outlines and display them on a triangular cardboard stand.

Activity 218 World weather

Materials needed
Slides of weather world-wide, pictures from magazines and travel brochures, world map.

Show the children some slides of weather in different parts of the world. Discuss the pictures. What can they tell about each place? Does it look cold or hot? Is it wet or dry? Would the children like to live there? Give them **Copymaster 109** (World Weather) to complete. In which part of the world would they expect to find these different weather conditions? Cut up some of the copymasters and pin the pictures to the correct part of the world map as part of a display on world weather. Add pictures from magazines and travel brochures.

Blueprints links
There is a section on the weather (sheets 91–102) in the *Infant Geography Resource Bank*. This covers weather charts, the seasons and weather in different parts of the world.

WATER ▶

Pupils should be given opportunities to investigate physical and human features of their surroundings.

Interpretation
The children should know that water occurs in the environment as rain, fog, clouds, ponds, rivers and seas: and that it freezes to create ice, hail, frost and snow. They also need to be aware of the effects of water on the landscape as it runs down slopes.

Progression indicators
● name a variety of places where water is found
● know how water is used in school and home
● recognise different forms of water

Introduction

Geographers are particularly interested in water because it covers so much of the Earth's surface. The processes of evaporation, condensation and precipitation account for the development of weather systems. Rivers and glaciers shape the landscape as they wear away rocks. All living creatures depend on water for their survival.

Water is a familiar part of children's lives. Not only is it essential for health and hygiene, it also features in many games and pastimes. Seaside holidays are especially popular, and many children enjoy playing in pools and puddles. It may surprise them to learn that water commonly occurs in the environment in three very different forms – liquid, gas and solid. The opportunities for links with science are particularly strong.

Key vocabulary

cloud	rain
drizzle	river
flood	sea
fog	slope
frost	snow
hail	steam
ice	water
lake	waterfall
pond	

Key questions

Where does water come from?
Does water run uphill?
How does water disappear from puddles?
Does ice always melt?
How do we use water?
What would we do without it?

Resources

Legends

Floods feature in many myths and legends. The most obvious is perhaps the story of Noah, which provides a good link with religious education.

Stories

There are a number of children's stories which deal with the effect of water on the environment. 'In Which Piglet is Entirely Surrounded by Water' from *The House at Pooh Corner* by A.A. Milne (Methuen, 1928) is a particularly good example and introduces a wide variety of geographical vocabulary.

Songs

Harlequin by David Gadsby and Beatrice Harrop (Black, 1981) is a rich source of songs about water. 'Snowflakes', 'Ho! Jack Frost', 'The Umbrella Man' and 'The Rain Song' are just some of the songs which pick up the idea of water in the environment.

Activity 219 Water experiments

Materials needed

Plastic cups, jugs, bottles, water wheel and other play equipment, Plasticine, sand trays, watering can, watering can roses.

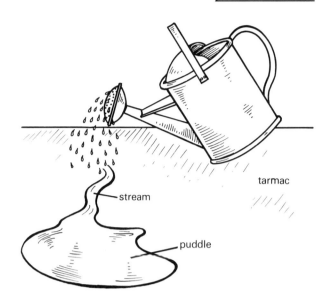

Fill a number of different containers with water. Does water have a special shape? Pour it down a tube onto a wheel. What happens? Does water always flow downhill? Working in a suitable part of the school grounds, pour water from a watering can to create 'raindrops'. See what happens when you change the watering can rose. Where does the water go as it reaches the ground? Are there any streams or miniature lakes? Try to create a dam and lake in a sand tray.

Activity 220 Word mobile

Materials needed

Card, scissors, coat hanger or gardening sticks, thread or string.

Make a mobile of water words. Write the words on pieces of card and arrange them in three groups: vapour words – fog, mist, cloud, steam; liquid words – rain, pond, river, sea; solid words – ice, hail, snow, frost. Suspend them from a coat hanger or frame made of gardening sticks, using thread or light string. You could add a two-dimensional globe to the centre of the mobile to emphasise that all the words describe the physical environment.

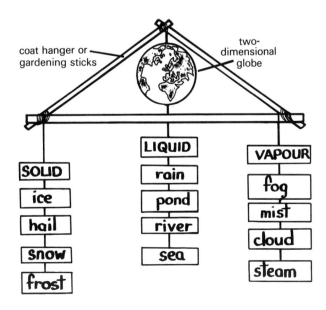

Activity 221 Water walk

Go for a water walk around your school to discover all the different things which are to do with water. Examples might include drainpipes, taps, drains, drinking fountains and puddles. Get the children to note down what they discover, either using **Copymaster 110** (Water Survey) or by making simple labelled sketches.

Activity 222 Playground quiz

Materials needed

Outline plan of the school playground.

Take the children into the playground and decide:

1 The best place to shelter from the rain.
2 The best place to see a pond or puddle.
3 The best place to make a slide in winter.
4 The best place to see flowing water.
5 The best place to see the most clouds.

Get the children to help you mark these different places on an outline plan while you are outside. Back in the classroom, the children should then write a few sen-tences about the places they have visited and pin their descriptions to the correct part of the plan.

Activity 223 Water and landscapes

Materials needed

Outline drawing and materials for class collage, photographs of different landscapes.

Make a large landscape collage showing water in lots of different forms. It could include clouds, streams, lakes, rivers, ponds, reservoirs, waterfalls and the sea. Get the children to write labels and pin them to the correct part of the collage. You might find it helpful to discuss photographs of different natural landscapes in order to develop their vocabulary. You could also reinforce the work by using the words for syllable clapping in music or associated language lessons such as poetry.

Activity 224 Round the world

Read the children an adventure story about a journey to a distant land. This might involve crossing oceans, fording rivers, travelling through woods and forests or

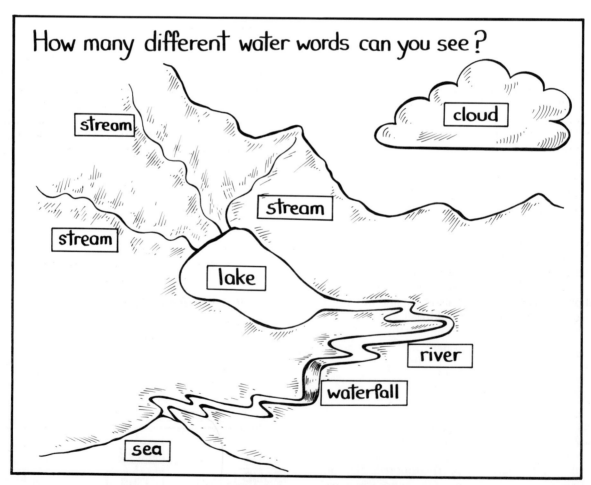

Water and landscapes. Get the children to pin labels to a landscape picture.

over mountains. *Percy Short and Cuthbert* by Susie Jenkin Pearce (Viking, 1990) is a good example. See if the children can draw a picture map to show the route taken. Make up a similar story with the children. Draw a map showing the route and naming some of the main landmarks. **Copymaster 111** (Sun and Showers) could be used to illustrate the idea of a story sequence.

84

Blueprints links
See copymasters 82–90 in the *Infant Geography Resource Bank* for a range of activities on water in the environment.

MATERIALS AND RESOURCES ▶

Pupils should be given opportunities to become aware that the world extends beyond their own locality.

Progression indicators
● identify stone, wood, brick and metal in the school environment
● know how different materials are obtained
● associate products with the materials from which they are made

Interpretation
The children should investigate the different materials used in their own locality. They should find out how they are obtained through quarrying, mining, forestry, fishing and farming.

Introduction
We depend on natural resources in many different ways. Our homes are built from stone, wood and clay, our clothes are derived from plants and animals, our food is the product of the soil. Many young children will be unaware of these links.

You could introduce the work by considering your own locality. Are there any mines or quarries near your school? If not, why not? Where is the nearest forestry plantation or fishing port? Have any children been there? You could then consider the processes by which materials are obtained. Children might investigate how a quarry works and how fish are caught. In addition, they should find out how different raw materials are brought to the place where they live. The coal merchant, fish shop and timber yard are the outlets at the end of a chain that leads back to an industrial source.

It is also instructive to undertake simple surveys in the classroom and school building. How many different things can the children find which are made from iron or oil? Some of the links between raw materials and the final products are highly sophisticated and will only be appreciated by a minority of children.

Key vocabulary

brick	materials
coal	mine
colliery	oil
country	port
factory	quarry
farm	rock
fish	sheep
food	stone
forest	trawler
lorry	wood

Key questions
What natural materials are used in the school and classroom?
How are different materials obtained?
Where do they come from?

What is the difference between renewable and non-renewable resources?

Resources
Picture books
If you want to focus on building materials you could read the children the story of 'The Three Little Pigs'. The first one made his home from straw, the second from wood and the third from stone. Alternatively, you might consider food. This is one of the themes in *The Tale of Peter Rabbit* by Beatrix Potter. The adventure begins when Peter Rabbit squeezes under the gate into Mr McGregor's garden.

Rhyme

If all the World were Paper

If all the world were paper,
And all the sea were ink,
And all the trees were bread and cheese,
What should we do for drink?

Baa, Baa, Black Sheep

Baa, baa, black sheep,
Have you any wool?
Yes, sir, yes, sir,
Three bags full:
One for the master,
And one for the dame,
And one for the little boy
Who lives down the lane.

Activity 225 Natural resources

Materials needed
A collection of natural resources, cardboard labels.

Make a collection of a variety of natural resources such as wood, stone, coal, sand, wool, cotton, leather, clay and oil. You could either provide all of these yourself or get the children to bring in items of their own from home. Write out a label for each one, talk about their origins and discuss why they are 'natural' resources. Get the children to put the labels in the right place. Take the labels away each morning before school and see if the children can replace them correctly. Use **Copymaster 112** (Material Puzzle) to consolidate the children's understanding.

Activity 226 Resources in the classroom

Do a survey of objects in the classroom. Discuss the natural resources that are used in each thing. Pin or stick labels on to the items with which they are associated. For example, a label saying wood should be fixed to the table, sand to the glass and clay to the bricks.

Activity 227 Resources and products mobile

Materials needed
Scissors, crayons, string, glue, cardboard.

Get the children to draw a picture of one type of natural resource and a picture of something that has been obtained from it. Examples might include milk from cows, metal from rocks and books from trees. Make a mobile by arranging the drawings in pairs. Put the resource at the top and the product underneath. You could use **Copymaster 113** (Resources Mobile) as a way of introducing the activity, or to help children who find it hard to think of examples to draw. You could extend the work by asking the children to make a mobile of all the things they can think of that are made of wood, wool or oil. Not only does this make an attractive classroom display, it also helps to highlight the properties of different natural resources.

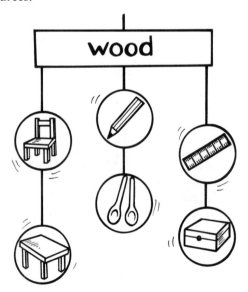

Activity 228 Wood rubbings

Materials needed
Large wax crayons, greaseproof paper.

Make a series of rubbings of wooden objects around your class and school. You could mount these as a display with labels saying what they show. If possible, take a photograph of each object and put it next to the appropriate rubbings. This will help to set them in context. Discuss the rubbings with the children and get

them to suggest suitable descriptive words, such as rough, smooth, swirling, straight. Extend the work using **Copymaster 114** (Trees are Wood).

Activity 229 Woollen clothes

Materials needed
Collection of woollen clothes, different types of wool.

Look at your collection of woollen clothing. Decide how it is possible to tell if the material is wool. The children might feel its texture, look at it carefully, check the label, look for the 'pure new wool' logo, and so on. Arrange for a weaver or knitter to come and talk to the children about what they do. If possible, contact a local farm and arrange for the children to see a sheep. This will introduce them to the 'resource' in a very practical and direct manner.

Activity 230 Miniature characters

Materials needed
Wool, rings of cardboard, buttons, glue.

Do some simple weaving with scraps of wool, or make a woollen ball which can be turned into a miniature character (see overleaf). Set up a market stall for the goods which the children have made. Design a package, cost the materials and find out a 'commercial price' for the products. Make an advertisement to encourage people to buy them.

Activity 231 Made of iron and steel

Materials needed
Magnets.

Go for a walk round your school to find materials made of iron. Give the children magnets so that they can carry out simple tests. They can record their results using **Copymaster 115** (Made of Iron and Steel). They could also take rubbings of any iron objects which have interesting patterns. When you return to the classroom make a list of all the objects the children have discovered and add this to a class display.

Activity 232 Zig-zag book

Materials needed
Reference books on iron and steel-making, hammers, nails, card, glue.

Make a storybook about the life of a nail. You will need reference books to find out how iron ore is dug out of the ground and made into steel in a furnace. Mount a number of different nails in the book. Write down how they are used. For example, small pins are used in picture frames while large masonry nails secure window and door frames. Find some hammers to go in a display with the book.

Activity 233 How are they obtained?

Discuss the different ways materials are obtained from the natural environment. Clay is *dug* out of the ground, stone is *cut* in quarries, coal is *mined* under the ground, crops are *harvested* on farms. Make a collection of the different words that describe these activities. Get the

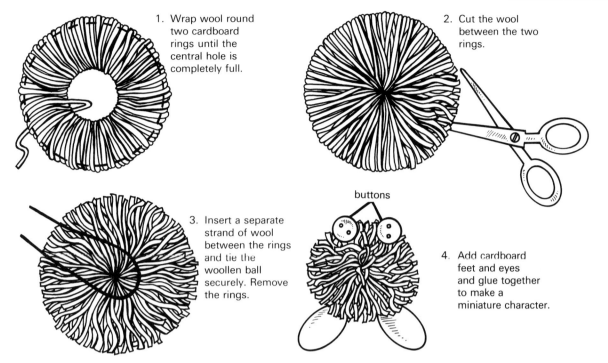

1. Wrap wool round two cardboard rings until the central hole is completely full.

2. Cut the wool between the two rings.

3. Insert a separate strand of wool between the rings and tie the woollen ball securely. Remove the rings.

buttons

4. Add cardboard feet and eyes and glue together to make a miniature character.

How to make miniature characters

children to complete **Copymaster 116** (Do they match?) and play a game of snap using the words and picture cards.

Activity 234 Different sources

Materials needed
Basic materials and equipment for artwork.

Make a survey of the classroom or school. Decide which items come from under the ground, which ones come from farms, which ones come from trees and which ones come from the sea. Get the children to draw pictures of different things in their survey and put them up as a wall display under these four different headings.

These things come from UNDER THE GROUND

rings   slates

These things come from THE SEA

fish   shells

These things come from TREES

pencil   box

These things come from FARMS

bread   milk

Different sources. Make a survey of everyday items.

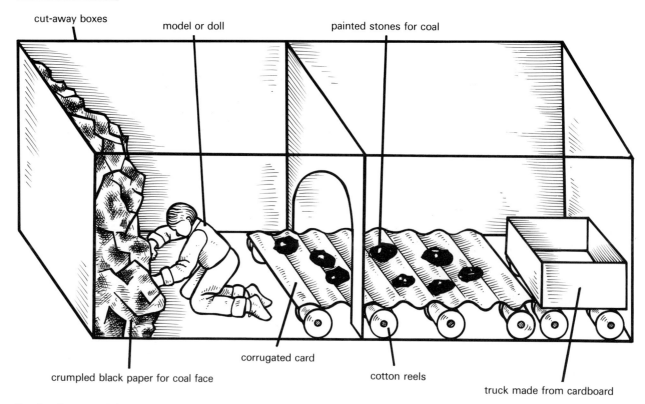

cut-away boxes

model or doll

painted stones for coal

crumpled black paper for coal face

corrugated card

cotton reels

truck made from cardboard

Coal mine model

Activity 235 Farming, fishing and mining

Talk about the people who earn their living obtaining materials from the environment. Examples include quarry workers, fishermen, farmers, miners and lumberjacks. Do the children know anybody who has one of these jobs? If possible, arrange for them to come and talk to the class, and get them to bring some tools and specialist equipment with them. Alternatively, you might be able to set up a small exhibition of people at work using posters and photographs. Some local museums have equipment which they are able to loan to schools on request.

Activity 236 Machines

Materials needed

Toy machines, models, plans of a port, quarry and farm.

Make a collection of models and toys that might be used in a port, quarry and farm. You will need tractors, combine harvesters, fishing boats, diggers, and so on. Get the children to group the toys into mini-scenes. When they are familiar with the toys you could extend the work by providing simple plans for the different sites. Keep the plans and toys in a box so that the children have to sort them into groups each time they use them. Check that they understand where the machines belong on the plans and encourage them to experiment with different arrangements. **Copymaster 117** (Machines) is designed to help children understand more about the machines and equipment used in extractive industries, and relates closely to this activity.

Activity 237 Underground scene

Materials needed

Posters and pictures of mines, old shoe boxes, black paper, corrugated card, cotton reels, cardboard, small dolls, fabric.

Find a poster or some photographs of a coal mine that you can use in a class display. Use this as the reference source for making a model of an underground scene. The children could join a couple of old shoe boxes together to make a tunnel, and fill one end with black paper to represent the coal face. Corrugated card is a simple way of giving the impression of a conveyor belt, and the coal can be made from painted pebbles. Complete the scene by adding a figure or two digging out the coal, and make a few simple trucks from cardboard to place at the other end.

Activity 238 Fishing fleet

Materials needed

Margarine tubs, cardboard, Sellotape, paint, pictures and photographs of fishing boats, netting.

Get the children to make some model fishing boats. They could use a margarine tub for the hull and make the bridge from cardboard and Sellotape. When they have finished, ask the children to paint their boats and give them each a name. Put the models on a cardboard base to make a fishing fleet and build harbour walls round the edge.

Collect postcards and photographs of fishing boats and add them to the display. Pin some netting to one of the corners and ask the children to paint and cut out some drawings of fish. Discuss what happens to fish when they are caught.

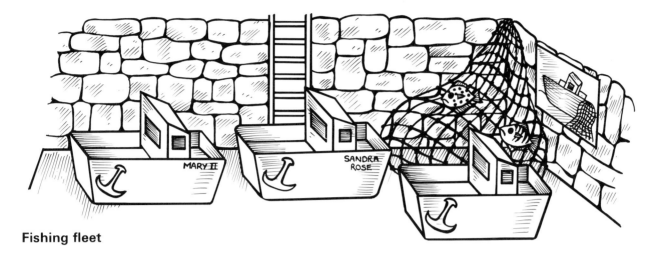

Fishing fleet

Activity 239 Fish mobile

Materials needed

Cardboard, hoop, light string, glue.

Make a mobile of fish in the sea with a trawler and net. Begin by asking the children to colour and cut out the fish in **Copymaster 118** (Fish). Glue the fish on to a strip of card as a frieze and cut the top in an undulating pattern to represent waves. Fix the card round a hoop and suspend the mobile from the ceiling using light string. Complete the display by adding a drawing of a trawler and a net.

Fish mobile

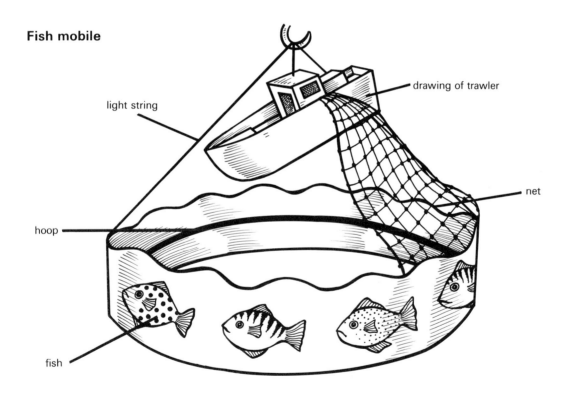

Blueprints links
The section on Making Things in the *Infant Geography Resource Bank* (sheets 41–68) provide a wealth of pictorial information about how common products are obtained including milk, strawberries, fish fingers, coal, wool and bricks.

USEFUL ADDRESSES

Aerial photographs
Hunting Aerofilms Ltd
Gate Studios
Station Road
Boreham Wood
Herts WD6 1EF
Tel: 0181 207 0666

Photo Air
Photo Air House,
191a Main Street,
Yaxley
Peterborough PE7 3LD
Tel: 01 733 241850

Atlases
Customer Services
Collins Longman Atlases
Longman Group UK Ltd
Harlow
Essex CM20 1BR
Tel: 01279 623888 or
0141 772 3200

Charts
Pictorial Charts Educational Trust
27 Kirchen Road
London W13 0TY
Tel: 0181 567 5343

Developing countries
ActionAid
Hamlyn House
Macdonald Road
London N19 5LP
Tel: 0171 281 4101

Catholic Fund for Overseas
Development (CAFOD)
162 Stockwell Road
London SW9 9TQ
Tel: 0171 733 7900

Worldaware
1 Catton Street
London WC1 4AB
Tel: 0171 831 3844

Christian Aid
35 Lower Marsh
London SE1 7RG
Tel: 0171 620 4444

Development Education Centre
Gillett Centre
998 Bristol Road, Selly Oak
Birmingham B29 6LE
Tel: 0121 472 3255

Oxfam
274 Banbury Road
Oxford OX2 7GZ
Tel: 01865 311311

Save the Children
Mary Datchelor House
17 Grove Lane
Camberwell
London SE5 8RD
Tel: 0171 703 5400

Environmental issues
Centre for Alternative Technology
Llwngern Quarry
Machynlleth
Powys SY20 9AZ
Tel: 01654 703743

Friends of the Earth
26 Underwood Street
London N1 7JQ
Tel: 0171 490 1555

Greenpeace
Canonbury Villas
London N1 2HB
Tel: 0171 354 5100

World Wide Fund for Nature
Weyside Park
Godalming
Surrey GU17 1XR
Tel: 01483 426444

Globes and compasses
N.E.S. Arnold
17 Ludlow Hill Road
West Bridgfield
Nottingham NG2 6HD
Tel: 0115 945 2201

Hope Education
Orb Mill
Huddersfield Road
Waterhead
Oldham OL4 2ST
Tel: 0161 633 6611

Inflatable globes
Cambridge Publishing Services Ltd
PO Box 62
Cambridge CB3 9NA

Journals
Primary Geographer
Geographical Association
343 Fulwood Road
Sheffield S10 3BP
Tel: 0114 267 0666

Maps
Information and Publications
Ordnance Survey
Romsey Road
Southampton SO9 4DH
Tel: 01703 792000

Satellite Images
M.J.P. Geopacks
PO Box 23
St. Just
Penzance
Cornwall TR19 7JS
Tel: 01736 787808

National Remote Sensing Centre
Arthur Street
Barwell
Leicestershire LE9 8GZ
Tel: 01455 841785

Television
Educational Television Trust
PO Box 100
Warwick CV34 6TZ